101 Original
INSPIRATIONAL QUOTES
That Make You Think

101 Original INSPIRATIONAL QUOTES That Make You Think

Guiding Principles & Life Philosophy for Critical Thinking and Analysis

For Leaders and Decision-Makers

Andrea Campbell

Pocket Learner Publishing

Copyright ©2023 by Andrea Campbell. All rights reserved.

The content contained within this book may not be reproduced, duplicated, or transmitted without the author's or publisher's direct written permission available from andrea@andreacampbell.co.uk
Website: https://andreacampbell.co.uk

Legal Notice:
This copyright-protected book is intended only for personal use.

Disclaimer Notice:
The information is only for educational and entertainment purposes. No warranties of any kind are declared or implied. By reading this document, the reader agrees that under no circumstances is the author responsible for any direct or indirect losses incurred due to the use of the information contained herein, including, but not limited to, errors, omissions, or inaccuracies.

ISBN: 978-1-914997-40-2 (sc)   978-1-914997-41-9 (hc)

I would like to thank my family Richmond and Shari
for their inspiration, understanding, and patience.

Thanks also to my grandmother, Mrs. Iris
Ingram Steele, who inspired me to live my life
in the pursuit of excellence, with gratitude,
and in the service of others.

Thanks also to Caroline Hurry and David White,
my mastermind colleagues, who share with grace
during our weekly sessions and beyond.
I appreciate you!

If you like this content and want to receive our newsletters and be informed of new releases, please join our mailing list by clicking the link below or scanning the QR Code.

As a thank you for signing up, you can download a set of original inspirational posters that you can print, frame, and position in your favorite space.

http://eepurl.com/h8SU31

Please leave me a review

I'd also like to take the opportunity to ask you to leave me a review if you like this book. Reviews are very important to authors; they help our books to rank on the various platforms, and thus be more visible to readers. Thanks for your support.

PREFACE

Welcome to the world of "101 Original Inspirational Quotes That Make You Think." You're about to embark on a transformative journey that invites you to explore the depths of your thoughts, question your assumptions, and embrace the power of original wisdom. This book is an invitation to engage in a dialogue with yourself. It's an opportunity to challenge your perspectives, cultivate self-awareness, and refine your approach to leadership and decision-making. It's a call to action to infuse your life with purpose, empathy, and authenticity.

These divinely inspired quotes are seeds to plant, ponder, and nurture. Read them with an open heart and a curious mind. Use them as catalysts for personal reflection and critical thinking. Carry them in your thoughts and implement them in your actions. Let them stimulate your creative, analytical mind and inspire you with wisdom. Share and use them to design a more empowered future. Use these insights as leadership tools to strengthen your relationships and decision-making.

Wisdom is not confined to the pages of ancient texts or the lips of famous figures. It's a living force born from our unique experiences, introspection, and the moments of clarity that shape our lives. The quotes in this book are a testament to this belief.

You author your own story, and each day presents new opportunities. Embrace each moment, face every obstacle, and savor each triumph with the spirit of empowerment that this book stirs within you. May this book serve as a source of inspiration and transformation on your journey toward becoming a more thoughtful, ethical, and purpose-driven leader. May it remind you that wisdom is not something external to be sought; it is a wellspring within each person, waiting to be discovered and shared.

These are transformative ideas that are easily read, but these words must not be confined to these pages. Life transformation happens when you reflect on the concepts and apply them to your circumstances for long-term impact.

Here's to a future illuminated by the brilliance of your creative, imaginative spirit.

TABLE OF CONTENTS

Introduction … … … … … … …   1

Chapter I – Examples … … … … …   5

Part I – Body … … … … … … …   47

Part II – Mind … … … … … … …   79

Part III – Spirit … … … … … …   113

Conclusion … … … … … … …   154

INTRODUCTION

This book, "101 Original Inspirational Quotes That Make You Think," is part of my journey of introspection and inspiration. On these pages, you'll find quotes that touch upon various facets of life—managing challenges, nurturing relationships, harnessing resilience, and cultivating gratitude.

With every turn of the page, you'll encounter a new perspective that encourages you to ponder, question, reflect, and aspire. Each of these 101 thought-provoking and motivational quotes is a window into a world of wisdom, inviting you to delve into the depths of your thoughts, emotions, and experiences.

These pearls of wisdom are not mere creations of mine but conduits through which universal wisdom flows. It is an honor beyond measure to extend these insights with others, for they carry the potential to ignite transformation and provide illumination.

In the hustle and bustle of our daily lives, we often seek moments of clarity, guidance, and inspiration. This collection has been carefully curated to offer you just that—a diverse array of quotes that resonate with the human spirit, serving as beacons of light in times of uncertainty and sources of empowerment on the path to personal growth.

What makes these quotes exceptional is their holistic and inclusive nature. They can inspire critical thinking on varying levels and foster social cohesion, transcending barriers of academia, social standing, and economic status. Each quote is an invitation, beckoning you to think more profoundly.

The quotes provide insight that encourages contemplation, stimulates conversations, and inspires change. As you immerse yourself into the message encoded within each phrase, you may embark on a path of self-discovery. Some quotes are abstract, while others are relatively straightforward. Don't be deceived by the latter, for they all have the potential to unearth profound truths.

The quotes transcend time, culture, and circumstance. You can connect with universal truths that span generations. As you navigate through the pages, take a moment to consider the meanings and implications of each statement in the context of your personal and professional life.

Reflect on the paths you've trodden, lessons learned, and aspirations that guide your actions. Use the prompts outlined in the examples given to inspire your introspection as you work your way through the quotes.

The true magic of these insights unfolds in shared spaces. Gatherings—in the classroom, the boardroom, places of worship, or in the embrace of families and friends—are great settings to explore these quotes.

Ultimately, this book is an invitation to embark on a voyage of growth as a leader and decision-maker. Embrace the book as a companion on your journey, offering guidance, encouragement, and inspiration as required. May you be inspired as you navigate leadership challenges with resilience and gratitude, embracing the lessons learned with an open heart and an eager mind.

Prepare to explore, contemplate, and be uplifted as you embark on this enriching odyssey through 101 inspirational quotes—a testament to the enduring power of words to transform, uplift, and illuminate. These quotes are not mere words; they are keys to unlocking creativity and analytical skills for successful leadership and decision-making.

In my coaching role, I have used the quotes successfully to inspire people in their personal and professional pursuits. Their impact reverberates deeply, prompting personal reflection and enrichment as well as initiating positive change and holistic growth.

This impact resonates deeply within my own story as well. When I held my newly-born child and was informed of her unique challenges, despair clouded my horizon. Yet, through time, a glimmer of light emerged as she triumphed over her developmental milestones, each victory a testament to the quote, "No matter how vast the darkness, the tiniest of lights will penetrate it." This message became my beacon, guiding me through uncertainty to a place of empowerment. (This quote is not in this book; it is listed in my earlier book titled "Empowered.")

From this transformative experience emerged a commitment to empower families to uplift their children who face learning challenges and associated disabilities. My mission, which I may not have embraced without this experience, has borne fruit through my books and the creation of an innovative, award-winning educational development system called the Pocket Learner. The program empowers families and shines a light on children with special needs, impacting families far and wide.

The 101 quotes are part of a broader compilation nurtured over several years. This book is the second in the series; the first book is titled "Empowered," containing 120 of my unique inspirational quotes. As you approach these quotes, please do so with an open mind. Some will appeal to you more than others. Use them as mirrors to reflect the light within you as you make sense of your reality. Use these insights to reassure you, comfort, and inspire you to overcome uncertainty and rise above adversity in your leadership role.

Everyone is a leader at some point. We all have to make decisions that impact others and ourselves. At the very least, we are leaders of ourselves. As you progress through this book, may you discover your innate wisdom, joy, and creativity. And as you allow these words to weave into your life, may you become an agent of transformation, propagating positivity and enlightenment to all those you touch.

Thank you for engaging with these quotes. As the words reverberate, may they ignite the flames of leadership, critical thinking, and transformative growth that empower you to share your innate gifts with those you touch. May you find this book a worthy companion that inspires you daily.

Chapter 1: EXAMPLES

In this chapter, I presented my exploration into three of the quotes. I have dissected them and provided examples of how they might be interpreted and explored. Two examples are based on abstract quotes, while the third is somewhat straight-forward.

I have added this chapter not as a prescription but as a source of inspiration to help you explore and motivate you to engage and unleash your creative mind. I am keen for you to appreciate that these quotes, including the ones that appear simplistic, can be used for in-depth analysis. While reading and acknowledging them is acceptable, it may be more beneficial if you look for deeper meanings. Approach them with an open mind, considering the various angles from which they might be interpreted.

Think about how people from different cultures and backgrounds may interpret them. There may be cases where you disagree with them; that is valid too, for while everyone's opinion may vary, the truth remains the same.

As leaders and decision-makers, we manage and interact with people from all walks of life. Using these quotes is a valid way to unearth universal truths. They provide a creative means of understanding thought processes—a skill that can improve leadership prowess.

Example Quote No. 1: *"The doctor has the medicine, and the medicine has the doctor."*

This thought-provoking statement delves into the intricate relationship between individuals and the external factors that influence them. This quote invites us to explore the dynamic interplay between personal agency and external influences, high-lighting the idea that just as individuals possess the ability to influence their environment, the environment, in turn, can shape individuals.

As you dissect this quote, put yourself in the doctor's place and think about the "medicine" you are administering and to whom. Consider yourself as the patient and think about the "medicine" you are taking and who is prescribing this "medicine." Is this "medicine" bitter or is it sweet? Has it helped you? Are you still taking it? Did you learn anything from the experience? Think also about who's got your back and vice versa. Conversely, consider who's "got" you when really you thought you had the advantage. Let's delve into other potential interpretations of this quote.

Mutual Dependency and Balance: The quote suggests a symbiotic relationship between two seemingly distinct entities: the doctor and the medicine. This relationship can be seen as a metaphor for the intricate balance between our internal selves and the external world. As a doctor provides healing through medicine, we interact with our surroundings to find sustenance, growth, and well-being. This interpretation prompts us to reflect on the importance of maintaining equilibrium between our actions and our environment.

Reflection of Identity: The quote invites us to ponder the elements of our identity that are deeply intertwined with external influences. This could include our cultural heritage, upbringing, education, and experiences. By recognizing these external threads, we gain insight into the complex mosaic of who we are and the multifaceted sources that contribute to our sense of self.

The Power of Environment: The quote highlights the notion that our environment can shape us just as much as we shape it. This can extend to physical surroundings, social contexts, and even the digital realm. By acknowledging the impact of our environment, we become more conscious of the spaces we inhabit and their potential to either support or hinder our personal growth and development.

Internal and External Harmony: The quote encourages introspection into the elements influencing our lives. It prompts us to ask ourselves: What internal attributes or qualities shape our actions, decisions, and perceptions? Similarly, what external factors, such as culture, society, and relationships, influence our thoughts and behaviors? Exploring this balance can lead to a deeper understanding of how we align our internal selves with external circumstances.

Personal Transformation: Consider the idea that just as medicine has the potential to heal and transform, various experiences and encounters in our lives can bring about profound changes in our outlook, beliefs, and behaviors. Reflect on instances where you've undergone personal transformation due to impactful events or interactions.

Empowerment and Choice: While the quote emphasizes the influence of external factors, it also underscores the inherent agency of individuals. Just as a doctor administers medicine intentionally, we can make choices and take actions that contribute to our growth and well-being. This interpretation encourages us to recognize our capacity to shape our lives while navigating external influences.

Interconnectedness of Humanity: Expanding the quote's scope, we can view it as a representation of the interconnectedness of all human beings. Much like a doctor and medicine are inseparable, individuals are interconnected within the fabric of society. Our actions and choices ripple through the collective experience, emphasizing our shared responsibility to contribute positively to the well-being of others.

Mindfulness and Self-Awareness: The quote invites us to cultivate mindfulness and self-awareness in our interactions with the world. By understanding the reciprocal relationship between the doctor and the medicine, we can become more attuned to how external influences impact our thoughts, emotions, and behaviors. This awareness empowers us to make intentional choices that align with our values and aspirations.

Holistic Well-being: Building on the metaphor of the doctor and medicine, the quote encourages us to consider holistic well-being. Just as a doctor administers medicine to heal physical ailments, we must also recognize the importance of tending to our mental, emotional, and spiritual health. This interpretation prompts us to reflect on the "medicine" we provide ourselves through self-care, positive thoughts, and meaningful connections.

Lifelong Learning and Growth: The quote can be seen as a reminder of the continuous cycle of learning and growth. In a world of constant change, the "medicine" of knowledge, experience, and insight fuels our ongoing development. As the doctor prescribes the appropriate treatment, we must actively seek opportunities for learning and personal evolution to enrich our lives and contribute positively to the world.

Adapting to Circumstances: Just as a doctor adapts treatment plans based on a patient's condition, we should embrace flexibility and adaptability in response to life's challenges. The quote encourages us to assess our circumstances and make adjustments, recognizing that external influences and our choices shape our decisions.

Cultivating Resilience: The relationship between the doctor and medicine can symbolize resilience. In the same way a doctor perseveres in seeking the best treatment, we are called to develop resilience in the face of adversity. By acknowledging the reciprocal influence between inner strength and external challenges, we can harness our resilience to overcome obstacles and emerge stronger.

Examining Motivations: The quote invites us to examine our motivations and intentions. Why do we seek certain "medicines?" Are our choices aligned with our true desires and values, or are they influenced by external pressures? This introspection prompts us to make conscious decisions, contributing to our well-being and personal fulfillment.

Ethics and Morality: Delving more deeply, the quote touches on ethics and morality. Just as a doctor upholds the responsibility to use medicine for healing, we have a moral duty to use our abilities and resources responsibly and ethically. This interpretation encourages us to consider the impact of our actions on others and society as a whole.

Legacy and Impact: The concept of the doctor and medicine also relates to the idea of leaving a legacy. Just as a doctor's expertise can impact a patient's well-being, our actions can potentially leave a lasting imprint on the lives of others and the world. Contemplating this interpretation encourages us to strive for actions that contribute positively to the lives of those around us.

Mind-Body Connection: The doctor and medicine metaphor can symbolize the mind-body connection. Just as medicine can impact physical health, our thoughts, emotions, and mental well-being influence our overall state. This interpretation emphasizes the importance of nurturing physical and mental health for a balanced and fulfilling life.

A Call to Conscious Living: Ultimately, the quote calls for conscious living. By recognizing the reciprocal relationship between our choices and external influences, we become more attuned to the impact of our actions. This awareness empowers us to live intentionally, making choices that align with our values and contribute positively to ourselves and the world.

Exploration of Purpose: Reflecting on the quote, we can embark on a journey of self-discovery and purpose. What "medicine" resonates deeply with us? What passions, talents, or causes drive us to take action? We can find greater fulfillment and meaning by aligning ourselves with our purpose.

Global Perspective: We can apply the quote to global challenges by expanding the context. Just as a doctor addresses health issues, humanity must address pressing global concerns like climate change, social inequality, and healthcare access. This interpretation underscores our collective responsibility to contribute solutions for a better world.

*** *** ***

The quote prompts us to explore the intricate balance between our agency and the external influences that shape us. It encourages us to consider the various aspects of our identity, the power of environment, and the dynamic relationship between personal growth and the world around us.

With this quote, we embark on a journey of self-discovery, self-awareness, and empowerment, ultimately leading to a deeper understanding of what truly has us and how we, in turn, influence the world. In addition, the quote prompts us to explore myriad profound concepts—from holistic well-being and resilience to ethics, purpose, and global responsibility. It encourages us to make intentional choices that align with our values, aspirations, and the betterment of society.

As we evolve in our roles as leaders, thinkers, and decision-makers, we must never lose sight of the need for emotional intelligence and critical thinking. Embrace lifelong learning to continuously develop and lead yourself before you can lead others effectively.

Considerations and Reflections

1. How do you interpret the quote "The doctor has the medicine and the medicine has the doctor" in your own words?

2. How do external factors, such as culture, upbringing, and environment, shape your identity and sense of self?

3. Reflect on a time when an external factor or experience influenced a significant change in your perspective, behavior, or decisions.

4. Can you identify a specific "medicine" that has significantly influenced your beliefs, values, or aspirations? How has this impacted you?

5. How do you balance your agency with global influences?

6. Discuss strategies for harnessing your own inner strength as a "doctor" to overcome adversity.

7. How can being mindful of your intentions lead to more intentional outcomes?

8. How can aligning your actions with your intentions lead to a sense of harmony and purpose?

9. Can you recall an experience where a "medicine" in the form of knowledge, advice, or insight led to personal growth or transformation?

10. How can you use your personal "medicine" to positively impact others and contribute to the well-being of our communities?

11. How can the concept of the doctor and the medicine be applied to overcoming challenges and setbacks in your life?

12. Can you recall an example of a situation where you had to make a decision while considering both your personal choices and external factors?

13. How can the continuous pursuit of learning be a powerful "medicine" in your journey of self-improvement and professional development?

14. How can the metaphor of the doctor and the medicine highlight your ethical responsibilities in using your influence and resources?

15. How does the quote reflect the interconnectedness between your mental, emotional, and physical well-being?

16. Explore practices that nurture both your mind and body, recognizing their reciprocal relationship.

17. Reflect on the passions, talents, or causes that resonate with you as a potential source of your personal 'medicine.'

18. Give an example of a person, historical figure, or role model whose "medicine" inspires and influences you.

19. How can the quote be applied to addressing global challenges? How can you be both "doctor" and "medicine" in creating positive change on a larger scale?

20. Consider how you can contribute to solving societal and environmental issues through conscious actions.

21. How can the concept of the doctor and the medicine guide you in discovering and defining your life's purpose?

22. Reflect on the legacy you want to leave behind. How can your actions serve as a positive "medicine" for future generations?

Workshop/Group Exercises

The following questions can be used to spark meaningful discussions during your workshop. They encourage participants to explore their experiences, beliefs, and aspirations related to the quote, fostering a deeper understanding of the concept and its potential implications.

These considerations offer diverse avenues for exploration and motivate participants to engage in self-analysis, share personal experiences, and collaborate in meaningful conversations. Studying these questions enables you to facilitate rich and dynamic interactive workshop experiences that delve deeply into the layers of meaning encapsulated within each quote.

1. Brainstorm practical ways you can apply the insights from the quote in your daily life.

2. Set a personal goal for integrating the concept of the doctor and the medicine into your decision-making and interactions.

3. Reflect on patterns or cycles in your life where external factors have influenced your choices and behaviors. How can awareness of these patterns empower you to make more conscious decisions?

4. How can the quote inspire you to embody the changes you wish to see in the world? How might your actions serve as a positive "medicine" to inspire others to follow suit?

5. What are the symbolic "medicines" that contribute to your well-being? These could be hobbies, passions, relationships, or practices that positively impact your life.

6. Share an experience where you empathized with someone whose perspective differed from yours. How can empathy be a potent medicine for building bridges and fostering under-standing?

7. Reflect on the therapeutic power of nature. How does spending time in natural settings serve as a "medicine" for your well-being, influencing your mood, creativity, and overall health?

8. How can you consciously create positive feedback loops between your actions and their outcomes? How might nurturing these loops contribute to sustained personal development?

9. Reflect on the changing nature of your relationships with external influences. How have these relationships evolved, and what insights can you glean from these transformations?

10. How does the "medicine" of personal and collective storytelling shape your identity and cultural perspectives? How can sharing narratives promote understanding and empathy?

11. Share a situation where you broke free from external limitations imposed by circumstances or others. How can this experience inspire you to be the "doctor" of your own growth?

12. Think of someone who has served as a "medicine" in your life, inspiring growth and positive change. How did their influence shape your journey, and how can you cultivate similar positive influences for others?

13. Reflect on a goal or intention you have. How can you use the wisdom of the quote to guide your actions and decisions as you work toward achieving that goal?

14. How can practicing gratitude be a powerful "medicine" that enhances your overall well-being and perspective on life? How might it influence your interactions with others?

15. Explore assumptions you hold about external influences. How have these assumptions shaped your perceptions, and how might they limit your growth potential?

16. How can you integrate the diverse "medicines" of different cultures, philosophies, and perspectives into your life? How might this integration contribute to a richer understanding of yourself and the world?

17. Explore practices that encourage self-reflection, such as journaling, meditation, or mindfulness. How can these practices function as your personal "medicine" for self-awareness and growth?

18. Envision the legacy you want to leave behind. How can you use the concept of the doctor and the medicine to craft a legacy of positive influence and meaningful contributions?

19. Reflect on a time when you embraced vulnerability, allowing external influences to contribute to your personal growth. How might vulnerability be a "medicine" for deeper connections and understanding?

20. How does the quote resonate with the concept of self-care? How can you be both the "doctor" and the "medicine" for your own well-being through compassionate practices?

21. How does the quote encompass paradoxical elements, such as control and surrender, influence and receptivity? How might embracing these paradoxes enhance your approach to life?

22. Discuss how individuals in positions of influence, such as leaders or mentors, can impact the lives of others through their actions and decisions. How can they be "doctors" of positive change?

23. Reflect on a past challenge that ultimately brought valuable lessons and growth. How did this experience demonstrate the relationship between adversity and personal development?

24. Share an example of a change you've wanted to make. How can the resilience you've developed serve as a "medicine" to help you overcome obstacles and achieve your goal?

25. Reflect on how setting healthy boundaries can act as a protective "medicine" against negative external influences. How can you ensure that your boundaries align with your values and aspirations?

26. Reflect on how subconscious beliefs and biases might influence your choices and interactions. How can self-awareness serve as a "medicine" for uncovering and reshaping these influences?

27. How can adopting a growth mindset—where challenges are seen as opportunities—be a transformative "medicine" in your pursuit of continuous self-improvement?

28. How can the "medicine" of resilience help you navigate challenges and setbacks? Reflect on a time when your resilience led to growth despite adverse circumstances.

29. Share an experience where you initially resisted a particular "medicine" but later embraced it, leading to positive transformation. How can this mindset of openness apply to other areas of your life?

30. Consider your relationships with others. How might the quote apply to your interactions, conflicts, and connections? How can you be a positive "medicine" in the lives of those around you?

31. How can creative outlets, such as art, writing, or music, serve as therapeutic "medicines" for emotional healing and self-expression?

32. Share a pivotal moment where an external factor acted as a catalyst for significant personal change. How did this experience shape your journey and perspective moving forward?

33. How do your perceptions of external influences shape your reality? How can shifting your perspective on these influences lead to a more empowered and fulfilling life?

34. Share an instance where curiosity led you to explore new perspectives or ideas. How can the "medicine" of curiosity expand your understanding and open doors to new possibilities?

35. How can you use the quote to reinforce positive habits that contribute to your well-being? How might these habits, in turn, shape your overall sense of self?

36. Consider seeking advice from mentors in your life. How have their experiences and insights acted as valuable "medicine" to guide your decisions?

37. How can leaders embody the principles of the quote to inspire and guide their teams or communities? How might they cultivate a culture that honors the reciprocal relationship between influence and impact?

38. Share wisdom or insight you've gained from the older generation. How can intergenerational exchange serve as a transformative "medicine" for mutual learning and growth?

39. Reflect on the cyclical nature of change and growth. How can understanding these cycles serve as a guiding "medicine" for embracing life's transitions with grace?

40. How can the quote relate to the healing power of human connection and empathy? How can you be a "medicine" for someone needing understanding and support?

Example Quote No. 2: *"You can't use heart surgery to treat a head injury."*

The above quote conveys a powerful metaphorical message that underscores the idea that different situations and challenges in life require different approaches and perspectives. It draws attention to the inherent distinction between matters of the heart and matters of the mind, suggesting that attempting to apply the wrong approach to a given situation can lead to ineffective or counterproductive outcomes.

This quote encourages us to recognize the importance of discerning when to engage our emotions and when to engage our rationality and how finding the appropriate balance between the two is critical to navigating life's complexities. Let's explore the quote further.

Balancing Emotion and Reason: The quote emphasizes balancing emotional sensitivity and logical reasoning. Just as heart surgery requires a precise and calculated approach, certain situations demand a rational, analytical mindset. On the other hand, matters of the heart often necessitate empathy, compassion, and a deep understanding of emotions.

Effective Communication: The quote underscores the significance of effective communication. Recognizing when to convey empathy and emotional support versus providing factual information can enhance conversation understanding and connection.

Leadership and Decision-Making: Effective leadership requires recognizing when to lead with empathy and when to make tough decisions based on data and strategy. Balancing these elements fosters trust and clarity.

Navigating Personal Relationships: In personal relationships, the quote highlights the need to approach each interaction considering both emotional and rational aspects. Misunderstandings can arise when one person focuses solely on logical arguments while the other seeks emotional validation or connection.

Embracing Emotional Intelligence: The quote underscores the value of emotional intelligence—the ability to recognize, understand, and manage emotions in ourselves and others. It suggests that effective problem-solving and decision-making require not only intellectual acumen but also an awareness of our own feelings and those of others involved.

Making Informed Choices: The quote encourages us to make informed choices by assessing the situation. Some decisions require careful evaluation of facts and data, while others may hinge on our personal values, beliefs, and feelings.

Conflict Resolution: When conflicts arise, the quote suggests that successful resolution involves addressing the factual aspects of the disagreement and the underlying emotions and perspectives. Finding common ground often requires acknowledging and validating both sides of the equation.

Coping with Loss and Grief: When dealing with loss or grief, the quote emphasizes the importance of addressing both emotional pain and the need for coping strategies. It acknowledges that healing involves acknowledging and honoring the emotional aspects of the experience.

Cultural and Social Understanding: In navigating cultural or social differences, the quote underscores the importance of respecting diverse viewpoints and understanding the emotional and intellectual contexts that shape them.

Intuition and Rationality: The quote highlights the synergy between intuition and rationality. Combining gut feelings and emotional insights with reasoned analysis can lead to well-rounded, holistic perspectives.

Cultivating Empathy and Understanding: The quote prompts us to cultivate empathy and understanding in a world often marked by divisions. Recognizing and addressing the emotional aspects of differing perspectives can foster connections and bridge gaps.

Personal Growth and Healing: The concept extends to personal growth and healing. A head injury necessitates specific medical treatment, while emotional wounds may require introspection, self-compassion, and seeking support to heal.

Relationship Building: The quote has relevance in building and maintaining relationships. It highlights the necessity of empathetic listening and understanding the emotional needs of those with whom we interact.

Inclusivity and Diversity: The quote underscores the importance of recognizing and respecting varying emotional responses and perspectives in diverse communities. Balancing these differences contributes to a more inclusive and empathetic society.

Conflict Resolution and Mediation: In conflict resolution, the quote guides us to acknowledge and address both parties' emotional experiences while working toward a fair and rational resolution.

Time and Healing: The quote suggests that some issues—especially those involving emotions—require time for healing and growth. Just as a head injury necessitates patience for recovery, emotional wounds may take time to mend.

Strategic Decision-Making: The concept extends to strategic decision-making. By acknowledging emotional and rational factors, leaders can make well-informed choices considering immediate and long-term implications.

Societal Issues and Policy: When addressing complex societal issues, the quote reminds us to consider both the emotional impact on individuals and the larger systemic changes required for practical solutions.

Parenting and Education: The quote offers guidance in parenting and education. Tailoring approaches based on a child's emotional needs and intellectual development foster growth and understanding.

Creativity and Innovation: The quote can be applied to creativity and innovation, emphasizing the role of intuitive insight (heart) and critical analysis (mind) in problem-solving and creative endeavors.

Boundaries and Self-Care: The quote encourages setting boundaries and practicing self-care. Recognizing when emotional involvement is draining or unproductive can help us prioritize our own well-being.

Personal Well-Being: The quote reminds us of the importance of self-care and self-awareness. Paying attention to our emotional and mental needs contributes to overall well-being.

Learning and Education: The quote highlights the value of fostering emotional intelligence alongside academic knowledge. Both are essential for well-rounded personal development.

Personal Values and Ethics: When making decisions aligned with personal values and ethics, the quote prompts us to assess how these choices resonate with our emotions and rational beliefs.

Respecting Individual Journeys: Applying the quote to personal growth, it encourages us to respect our unique journeys. Just as medical treatments are tailored to individual needs, our paths to self-discovery and development should honor our distinct emotional and intellectual landscapes.

Mindful Living: Applying the quote to mindful living, it invites us to engage fully in each moment by balancing our emotional experiences with present-moment awareness.

Mental Health Advocacy: The quote can be applied to mental health advocacy, reminding us of the need to offer empathy and understanding to individuals facing mental health challenges.

Cultivating Emotional Resilience: The quote highlights the importance of cultivating emotional resilience. Just as a head injury requires time and care, emotional strength is developed through self-awareness and support.

Spiritual and Philosophical Growth: The quote can extend to spiritual and philosophical growth, encouraging seekers to explore emotional and intellectual dimensions in their quest for understanding.

Artistic Expression and Creativity: In creative endeavors, the quote reminds artists to infuse their work with emotional depth and intellectual innovation, resulting in more impactful and meaningful creations.

Empowerment Through Self-Awareness: The quote emphasizes the importance of self-awareness. By recognizing whether a situation requires emotional sensitivity or analytical thinking, we empower ourselves to respond effectively.

Exploring Philosophy and Spirituality: Applying the quote to philosophical and spiritual exploration invites seekers to integrate emotional experiences with intellectual inquiry for a richer understanding of existence.

Crisis Management: The quote speaks to crisis management, emphasizing the importance of addressing immediate emotional needs while implementing practical solutions.

Embracing Vulnerability: The quote invites us to embrace vulnerability. Just as a surgeon's precision is required for heart surgery, the vulnerability in sharing our emotions can lead to deeper connections and mutual growth.

Harnessing Emotional Intelligence in Leadership: The quote underscores the value of emotional intelligence for leaders. Leading with empathy and understanding can foster employee engagement, collaboration, and overall organizational success.

Navigating Life Transitions: Applying the quote to life transitions—such as career changes or relocations—it guides us to honor the emotional impact of these shifts while making practical preparations.

The Art of Listening: The quote reminds us of the art of listening. We engage in more meaningful and effective communication by paying attention to spoken words as well as underlying emotions.

Promoting Social Change: In advocating for social change, the quote shows the importance of addressing emotional and systemic dimensions to create a lasting impact.

Building Authentic Relationships: In building relationships, the quote encourages authenticity. When we share our thoughts and emotions openly, we create a foundation for genuine connections.

Cultural Competence: The quote extends to cultural competence. Understanding the emotional nuances of different cultures allows us to engage respectfully and foster harmonious interactions.

Strengthening Resilience in Children: The quote has implications for parenting and education. Teaching children to recognize and manage their emotions alongside academic learning equips them with well-rounded tools for resilience.

Nurturing Creativity and Innovation: The quote inspires a multidimensional approach in creative fields. Nurturing both intuitive inspiration and analytical refinement can lead to innovative breakthroughs.

Supporting Mental Health Advocacy: The quote aligns with mental health advocacy. By acknowledging the emotional aspects of mental health challenges, we reduce stigma and promote compassionate support.

Celebrating Humanity's Complexity: Ultimately, the quote celebrates the complexity of the human experience. By embracing the intricacies of both heart and mind, we honor the depth and diversity of what it means to be human.

Empathy in Leadership: The quote emphasizes that effective leadership involves empathy. Leaders who understand the emotional needs of their team members can inspire trust and create a supportive work environment.

Reframing Negative Emotions: The quote suggests reframing negative emotions as signals for self-care. Just as pain denotes an injury, emotional discomfort prompts us to address underlying needs.

Navigating Ethical Dilemmas: The quote encourages us to consider emotional implications and rational consequences before making decisions when faced with ethical dilemmas.

Fostering Gratitude and Joy: The quote encourages us to nurture gratitude and joy. Recognizing emotional blessings alongside intellectual achievements leads to a more fulfilling and balanced life.

Enhancing Conflict Transformation: When engaging in conflict transformation, the quote guides us to approach disputes with empathy, acknowledging the emotional layers contributing to the situation.

Evolving Perspectives: Reflecting on the quote can lead to shifts in perspective. It encourages us to re-evaluate situations with a more balanced consideration of both heart and mind.

*** *** ***

This quote calls on you to recognize instances when your heart has ruled your head to your detriment. There may have been instances when someone tugged on your heartstrings, and you made decisions against your better judgment. Think about those moments and how you feel afterward, especially if there was a fallout from the decision.

Consider how it might have been different if you had listened to your inner voice, which whispered to you but which you had ignored. Think also about how you might have provided rational responses to situations where it might have been better to adopt a softer approach. Did you often have feelings of guilt or remorse?

Considerations and Reflections

1. How do you interpret the quote "You can't use heart surgery to treat a head injury" in your own words?

2. Consider an instance where your approach to a challenge differed due to recognizing the distinction between heart and mind. How did this awareness shape your actions?

3. Share a scenario where you had to make a decision requiring emotional understanding and rational analysis. How did you strike a balance between the heart and the mind?

4. Consider a time when you faced a challenge requiring emotional understanding and logical analysis. How did you manage this balance?

5. Recall a situation where emotions played a pivotal role in decision-making. How did this emotional aspect influence the outcome?

6. Consider a conflict resolution process where acknowledging emotional triggers and logical points led to a more harmonious resolution. How did this approach benefit all parties involved?

7. Think about a personal relationship where you had to address both emotional needs and practical concerns. How did you handle these different dimensions?

8. State how mindfulness can help you navigate daily life by balancing emotional experiences with present-moment awareness.

9. Consider a conflict you've been part of. How might acknowledging emotional triggers and logical points of contention lead to resolution?

10. State an experience where your vulnerability led to deeper connections. How did embracing vulnerability enhance both emotional and intellectual growth?

11. Consider a moment from your personal growth journey where embracing heart and mind was essential. How did this realization contribute to your development?

12. State an example of a decision where recognizing both emotional and rational implications was crucial for achieving your desired outcome.

13. State an instance when your emotional resilience helped you overcome a challenge. How did you also utilize your cognitive abilities to navigate the situation?

14. Consider a personal relationship where you successfully balanced emotional openness and intellectual growth. How did this balance contribute to the relationship's dynamics?

15. Consider a time when you applied the wisdom of the quote to address both emotional and practical aspects of a decision. How did this balanced approach influence the result?

16. Think about a time when you had to adapt to a significant change. How did you balance the emotional impact with practical adjustments?

17. Consider a personal value or belief requiring emotional conviction and logical justification. How do these two aspects complement each other?

18. Think of a personal experience where you witnessed the distinction between matters of the heart and matters of the mind?

19. Think about a situation where embracing heart and mind led to a deeper understanding of a complex issue. How did this understanding inform your actions or decisions?

20. Consider how the quote applies to your approach to parenting or education. How do you balance nurturing emotional well-being with fostering intellectual growth?

21. Consider a decision you made where recognizing the emotional and rational implications helped you confidently navigate uncertainty. How did this comprehensive understanding influence your path?

22. Think about a relationship in your life where understanding the other person's emotional needs was just as important as addressing practical matters. How did you navigate this balance?

23. Consider a situation where your emotional instincts guided you to make a decision. How did this emotional intuition align with the eventual outcome?

24. Consider an experience when your emotional responses contributed to a misunderstanding. How might introducing rational clarity have led to a more effective resolution?

25. State a personal accomplishment requiring emotional determination and intellectual skill. How did this synergy influence your achievement?

26. Think about a time when you had to make a decision involving emotional authenticity and rational considerations. How did this duality shape your choice?

27. State an instance when you embraced vulnerability, allowing emotional openness to lead to personal growth. How did this vulnerability enhance your overall development?

28. Consider a situation where your creative process was enriched by combining emotional inspiration with analytical refinement. How did this fusion elevate your creation?

29. State an example of an ethical dilemma where weighing emotional consequences alongside rational principles influenced your decision-making. How did this balance guide your choice?

30. Consider a personal practice that helps you maintain a balance between your emotional and intellectual well-being. How does this practice contribute to your overall equilibrium?

31. State an experience where your approach to a challenge transformed due to recognizing the importance of heart and mind integration. How did this transformation affect the outcome?

32. Think about a friendship that thrived because you honored emotional connections and shared intellectual interests.

33. State an instance where vulnerability paved the way for deeper connections with others. How did this emotional openness lead to more meaningful relationships?

34. Consider a situation where embracing emotional values and logical analysis was essential for making a significant decision. How did this dual approach contribute to your choice?

35. Share a moment from your personal growth journey where you recognized the need to balance your heart and mind. How did this realization contribute to your development?

36. State how embracing heart and mind contributes to your personal growth philosophy. How does this integration enhance your self-development journey?

37. State an example of a time when your awareness of a situation's emotional and rational aspects led to a more balanced perspective. How did this holistic view shape your actions?

38. How can the quote guide you in making ethical decisions that honor your emotional values and rational principles?

39. State an example of when you faced a challenging problem and had to rely on your emotional empathy and logical analysis to find a solution.

40. Think about a belief you hold that has both emotional conviction and logical justification. How do these two dimensions reinforce your understanding of this belief?

41. Consider how you balance nurturing emotional well-being with fostering intellectual growth as a parent or educator.

42. Share a significant life change you've experienced. How did you address the emotional impact while making practical adjustments?

Workshop/Group Exercises

1. Consider how acknowledging emotional nuances contributes to cultural understanding. How might this awareness bridge gaps between different perspectives?

2. Discuss how understanding a situation's emotional and intellectual context can lead to more effective problem-solving and

decision-making.

3. How does the quote relate to effective communication and empathy? How can considering both emotional and intellectual perspectives improve your interactions with others?

4. How can practicing mindfulness allow you to navigate the delicate dance between heart and mind in your daily life?

5. Reflect on a conflict you've been part of. How might acknowledging emotional triggers and logical points of contention lead to more constructive resolutions?

6. Describe your decision-making process. How do you incorporate your emotional responses and logical analysis to reach a conclusion?

7. Consider a conflict you've witnessed where acknowledging emotional motivations helped shed light on the underlying issues. How could understanding emotions lead to conflict resolution?

8. In parenting or education, how can you apply the wisdom of the quote to nurture both emotional well-being and intellectual growth in children?

9. How does the quote relate to cultural awareness and sensitivity? How might understanding emotional nuances help bridge gaps between cultures?

10. Discuss how influential leaders balance their emotional connection to their team members with strategic decision-making for the organization's success.

11. Share instances where you've needed to engage different aspects of yourself—emotionally and intellectually—in personal

and professional relationships. How did you navigate these situations?

12. State an example of a creative endeavor where emotional depth and analytical thinking intersected. How did this combination enhance the outcome?

13. Share an experience where your emotional resilience was crucial in overcoming a challenge. How did you also utilize your cognitive abilities?

14. Discuss the role of vulnerability in embracing both emotional openness and intellectual growth. How has vulnerability enriched your connections with others?

15. Apply the quote to societal issues. How can acknowledging and addressing emotional as well as intellectual aspects lead to more effective social change?

16. Consider a scenario where understanding emotional dynamics within a team led to improved collaboration and outcomes. How did this emotional intelligence enhance teamwork?

17. State how understanding emotional and rational aspects can lead to a more holistic perspective on personal growth and development.

18. How can the quote inspire creative thinkers and innovators to integrate emotional depth into their imaginative processes?

19. Consider a time when embracing emotional values and rational principles was necessary for ethical decision-making. How did this alignment impact your choice?

20. Consider a situation where acknowledging both emotional and

intellectual aspects could lead to more effective social change. How might this approach influence the outcome?

21. Think about a leader you admire who effectively balanced emotional connection with strategic decision-making. How did this equilibrium contribute to their effectiveness?

22. Consider a social or community issue where acknowledging emotional perspectives and logical solutions could lead to more sustainable change. How might this integration create impact?

23. State an experience where emotional intelligence improved communication and collaboration within a team or group setting. How did this enhance the overall outcome?

24. Think about a situation where vulnerability was key to embracing emotional openness and intellectual growth. How did this vulnerability impact your personal connections?

25. Consider a complex issue you approached using emotional and intellectual viewpoints. How did this dual consideration lead to a deeper understanding?

26. How does the quote relate to your personal definition of success and fulfillment? How can honoring both heart and mind lead to a more meaningful life?

27. How can emotional intelligence improve teamwork, communication, and conflict resolution within a professional setting?

28. Consider a situation where acknowledging emotional triggers alongside rational considerations resulted in more effective conflict resolution. How did this combined approach lead to a better resolution?

29. Consider a situation where a leader effectively balanced emotional connection with team members and strategic decision-making. How did this balance impact the team?

30. Discuss how understanding the quote can enhance relationships with family, friends, colleagues, or partners.

31. Reflect on the legacy you want to leave behind. How can embracing the wisdom of the quote shape your impact on others?

Example Quote No. 3: *"Sow where you don't expect to reap."*

The above quote holds layers of meaning and serves as a guiding principle for overcoming life challenges, pursuing unconventional pathways, and embracing the unknown with courage and resilience. This quote encourages us to venture beyond our comfort zones, challenge societal norms, and invest our efforts in places and endeavors that may not guarantee immediate or obvious rewards.

The quote carries a beautiful and meaningful message when applied to sowing into the lives of others without expectations. This interpretation emphasizes the act of selfless giving, nurturing, and supporting others purely for the sake of making a positive impact rather than seeking personal gain.

This quote advocates selflessness and attention to legacy. It goes beyond the duty to take care of our loved ones and ventures into the avenues of philanthropy. It entails being a global citizen who cares for causes outside oneself. Think about how it makes you feel when you help a stranger or when your organization fulfills its corporate social responsibility (CSR) to disadvantaged groups in your area or beyond. Do you have a CSR budget, and what impact is it making?

Do you get to see the difference you are making in the lives of others? Let's delve deeper into this quote and see what other applications it may have.

Pure Acts of Kindness: Sowing into the lives of others without expectations involves performing acts of compassion, kindness, and support with a genuine heart. It means extending a helping hand, offering guidance, or providing resources to uplift and empower others solely for the purpose of making their lives better.

Fostering Meaningful Relationships: When we sow into the lives of others without expecting anything in return, we cultivate authentic and meaningful relationships. These relation-ships are built on trust, mutual respect, and a shared commitment to one another's well-being rather than being transactional.

Creating Positive Ripples: Just as a single seed can lead to a flourishing garden, our selfless actions can create positive ripples that extend far beyond our initial efforts. By sowing into the lives of others, we contribute to a cycle of kindness and goodness, inspiring those we help to pay it forward and create a chain reaction of positive change.

Fostering Resilience and Patience: Sowing where we don't expect to reap teaches us the value of patience and resilience. Just as a farmer patiently nurtures the soil and tends to the crops, we must invest time and effort into areas that may not yield immediate results. This approach builds character, determination, and the ability to weather challenges, ultimately leading to a deeper appreciation for the fruits of our labor when they do eventually materialize.

Empowering Others: Sowing without expectations empowers individuals to realize their potential and achieve their goals. When we invest in the growth and development of others, we provide them with the tools, knowledge, and encouragement they need to overcome challenges and succeed.

Fulfillment through Giving: The act of sowing into the lives of others without expecting anything in return brings a sense of fulfillment and joy that transcends personal gain. It aligns with the principle that true happiness lies in enriching the lives of others and making a difference in their journeys.

Cultivating Gratitude and Appreciation: When we sow into the lives of others, we contribute to a culture of gratitude and appreciation. Those who receive our support are more likely to recognize and acknowledge the kindness they've experienced, fostering an atmosphere of positivity and thankfulness.

Embracing Risk and Uncertainty: At its core, this quote urges us to take calculated risks and explore uncharted territories. The greatest achievements and innovations are often born from stepping outside the familiar, where the outcomes are uncertain. By sowing our efforts where reaping seems unlikely, we open ourselves up to the possibility of unexpected and profound growth. This interpretation emphasizes the importance of embracing uncertainty and viewing it as a canvas for painting our potential.

Building a Strong Community: Selfless acts of sowing can contribute to forming stronger and more closely-knit communities. When individuals come together to support one another without ulterior motives, they create a sense of unity and shared purpose that benefits everyone involved.

Inspiring Transformation: Sowing without expectations has the potential to inspire transformative change in the lives of others. A simple act of encouragement or assistance can spark a profound shift in someone's perspective, choices, and trajectory, leading to a brighter and more hopeful future.

Leaving a Lasting Legacy: Sowing into the lives of others leaves a lasting legacy of compassion and generosity. Even if we don't see the immediate impact of our actions, our positive influence on others can carry forward through generations, leaving an indelible mark on the world.

Exemplifying Unconditional Love: Ultimately, sowing without expectations embodies the essence of unconditional love. It reflects a deep care for the well-being of others, a willingness to provide support without strings attached, and a belief in every individual's inherent worth and potential.

Breaking Conventional Boundaries: The quote challenges us to break free from conventional thinking and societal expectations. It encourages us to defy the limitations imposed by others or even ourselves. By daring to sow in unexpected places, we challenge the status quo, redefine possibilities, and pave the way for new perspectives and innovations.

Personal Growth and Self-Discovery: Sowing where reaping is uncertain can lead to profound self-discovery and personal growth. It prompts us to explore our own capabilities, passions, and potential in unexplored arenas. In this process, we uncover hidden talents, strengths, and aspects of ourselves that might have remained dormant otherwise.

Building Resilient Mindsets: The quote speaks to the importance of adopting a resilient mindset that thrives in adversity and remains undeterred by initial setbacks. Engaging in endeavors where the outcome is uncertain builds mental tough-ness and a capacity to adapt to changing circumstances, laying the foundation for enduring success.

Cultivating Empathy and Compassion: Sowing where reaping is not guaranteed can foster empathy and compassion.

When we invest in people, causes, or projects that may not yield immediate benefits, we connect with the struggles and aspirations of others on a deeper level. This empathy can lead to meaningful connections, collaborations, and a broader sense of purpose.

Inspiring Others through Example: Choosing to sow in unexpected places can inspire others to pursue their own unconventional paths. By demonstrating the value of resilience, courage, and determination, we inspire those who seek to create change and leave a positive impact.

Seeking Fulfillment: This quote underscores the idea that fulfillment and satisfaction often come from the journey rather than solely from the end result. By embracing the process of sowing and nurturing, we find purpose and joy in our daily efforts, regardless of the immediate outcome.

*** *** ***

In a world often driven by personal gain and self-interest, the concept of sowing into others without expecting to reap personal rewards serves as a powerful reminder of the transformative impact of selflessness and genuine compassion. By embodying this principle, we contribute to a more empathetic, connected, and harmonious society, where each act of kindness and support enriches the lives of both the giver and the receiver.

Considerations and Reflections

1. Have you ever experienced someone sowing into your life without expecting anything in return? How did it make you feel?

2. Reflect on a time when you sowed into someone else's life without expectations. What was the outcome, and how did it impact you?

3. How does the concept of sowing into the lives of others without expectations align with your personal values and beliefs?

4. How does the act of sowing into the lives of others contribute to building stronger relationships and communities?

5. How does sowing into the lives of others contribute to their personal growth and empowerment?

6. What are some practical steps you can take to sow into the lives of others without expecting to reap immediate rewards?

7. Share an example of a time when someone sowed into your life and how it contributed to your own transformation or growth.

8. Share strategies for practicing selfless giving while ensuring one's needs are met.

9. In what areas of your life do you tend to set expectations before giving or helping others? How might your approach change if you were to sow without expectations?

10. Identify one specific person, cause, or community you can sow into, and outline a plan for how you intend to make a positive impact.

11. How can the concept of sowing without expectations be instilled in younger generations? What benefits might this approach bring to their personal development and the communities they are part of?

12. Imagine an example where an unexpected act of kindness or support resulted in a positive chain reaction.

13 In what ways does sowing where you don't expect to reap require individuals to step outside their comfort zones? How does this contribute to personal growth?

14. Can you recall when you ventured into unfamiliar territory to sow into the lives of others? How did this experience broaden your horizons?

15. How can adopting a mindset of sowing without expectations help individuals recognize hidden opportunities for making a positive impact in unexpected places?

16. Can you recall a situation where you initially believed there would be no benefit to sowing into a particular situation, but it led to unexpected positive outcomes?

17. How do you measure the success of your efforts when sowing without expecting to reap immediate rewards? What alter-native measures of success can be more meaningful in such cases?

18. Share an example of a situation where you were able to identify a unique opportunity to sow into the lives of others, even though it wasn't initially apparent.

19. Share a personal example of how an act of selfless giving led to a deeper understanding of someone else's perspective.

20. How does mindfulness play a role in sowing without expectations? How can individuals cultivate a mindful approach to their acts of giving and support?

21. Discuss how aligning your actions with these values can lead to a more fulfilling and meaningful life.

22. Share examples of meaningful milestones that can be acknowledged and celebrated as part of the journey.

Workshop/Group Exercises

1. Discuss how the practice of sowing without expectations might influence your decision-making process, both personally and professionally.

2. Share a scenario where your decision to sow into the lives of others led to a positive outcome, even though you initially didn't anticipate it.

3. How can embracing the idea of sowing without expecting to reap reshape and strengthen your personal values and sense of purpose?

4. Share stories of how the willingness to sow into unexpected areas allowed for graceful adaptation in the face of challenges.

5. Share strategies for maintaining resilience and a sense of purpose even in situations where the anticipated "reap" does not materialize.

6. How does the principle of sowing without expectations equip individuals with the flexibility and adaptability needed to navigate changing circumstances?

7. Explore the potential skepticism or doubts that may arise when sowing into situations with uncertain outcomes. How can individuals overcome these doubts to fully embrace the concept?

8. Share experiences of supporting a cause that resonates with you and how it has impacted both the cause and your sense of fulfillment.

9. Discuss the idea that the true success of sowing lies in the intention and effort behind the action rather than the immediate outcomes.

10. Share an example of a project or endeavor where a group collectively sowed into a cause, even though individual rewards were not the primary focus.

11. How can the practice of sowing without expectations be transformed into a habit that positively shapes your daily interactions and choices?

12. How can practicing the act of sowing into the lives of others enhance our ability to empathize with their experiences and challenges?

13. Explore the possibility of disappointment when sowing without expectations. How can individuals cope with the absence of immediate rewards and maintain a positive outlook?

14. How can the concept of sowing without expectations be applied to collaborative efforts and group initiatives? How might this approach enhance teamwork and synergy?

15. Discuss the idea that being fully present in the act of sowing enhances the quality and impact of our efforts.

16. How does sowing into the lives of others without expectations celebrate the diversity of human experiences and backgrounds?

17. What steps can individuals and communities take to ensure that the impact of their selfless actions endures over time?

18. How might the concept of sowing without expecting to reap help bridge generational gaps and foster intergenerational understanding?

19. How might the concept of sowing without expecting to reap apply to creating a lasting legacy or leaving a positive mark on the world?

20. Who are some historical or contemporary figures who embody the idea of sowing without expecting to reap? How have their actions inspired others to follow a similar path?

21. Share stories of historical figures, community leaders, or role models whose selfless actions continue to inspire and benefit others long after they are gone.

22. How can sowing into causes you believe in, without expectations of personal gain, contribute to advancing those causes?

23. What challenges or barriers might individuals face when trying to sow into the lives of others without expecting anything in return? How can these challenges be overcome?

24. Discuss strategies for cultivating trust in the process and focusing on the inherent value of selfless giving.

25. How can individuals strike a balance between sowing into the lives of others and taking care of their own well-being?

26. How can celebrating small victories along the way enhance the experience of sowing without expecting to reap? How might these celebrations reinforce a sense of purpose and motivation?

27. Reflect on the concept of leaving a legacy of altruism. How might sowing into the lives of others without expectations contribute to a lasting impact that extends beyond our lifetime?

28. Share experiences or insights highlighting how different generations can come together through selfless giving.

29. How can the idea of sowing without expecting to reap be a unifying force that transcends cultural, social, and geographical boundaries?

30. Discuss how this concept can be a powerful tool for building bridges and fostering understanding between diverse communities.

31. Discuss ways to integrate this mindset into your routine to create a lasting impact on your relationships and community.

32. Identify a role model or historical figure who embodies the idea of sowing without expecting to reap. How have this person's actions influenced your perspective on giving and impact?

33. Envision a world where everyone practiced sowing into the lives of others without expecting immediate rewards. How might this world be different, and what positive changes could it bring about?

Now that you have seen how the quotes can be interpreted, I hope you are inspired. Here are some ideas to maximize their impact and enhance your experience:

1. Embrace the Pause: When you encounter a quote that resonates with you, pause for a moment. Give yourself the gift of time to reflect on the meaning, its relevance to your life, and the emotions it evokes.

2. Question Assumptions: Explore different angles of a concept and challenge assumptions. Use the questions provided to help you.

3. Relate to Personal Experiences: Relate the quote to your own life experiences. Has a similar situation or feeling arisen in your journey? How does the quote shed light on those experiences?

4. Journal Your Thoughts: Keep a journal or notebook alongside your reading to document your reflections, questions, and insights.

5. Share with others: Engage in discussions about the quotes with others. Their perspectives can offer fresh insights and broaden understanding of the quotes' implications.

6. Apply to Real-Life Scenarios: Consider how the wisdom in the quotes can be applied. Challenge yourself to integrate the principles into your decision-making, problem-solving, and interactions.

7. Practice Mindfulness and Meditation: Immerse yourself fully in the moment, absorbing the quote's essence without distractions. Take moments of quiet reflection to meditate on them; let the lessons seep into your consciousness.

8. Track Your Growth: Keep track of your personal growth as you engage with the quotes. How have your perspectives evolved? What positive changes have you noticed in your thinking and actions?

Enjoy!

Part I – BODY

The body represents the physical aspect of our being. It encompasses all the tangible and biological elements that make up a person. Our sensory experiences, physical sensations, and interactions with the external world are all mediated through the body. It's the vessel that enables us to engage with the material world and express ourselves physically.

Physical well-being affects mental and spiritual well-being: Physical health directly influences mental clarity and emotional stability. Taking care of our bodies through exercise, proper nutrition, and rest can positively impact our mental state and enhance our capacity for spiritual experiences.

The concept of being composed of body, mind, and spirit is a philosophical and holistic perspective on human nature that has been explored for centuries. This view emphasizes the interconnectedness and integration of various aspects of our existence.

A person with one foot in the water won't come to your rescue if you're drowning

A piglet can't teach an eaglet to fly

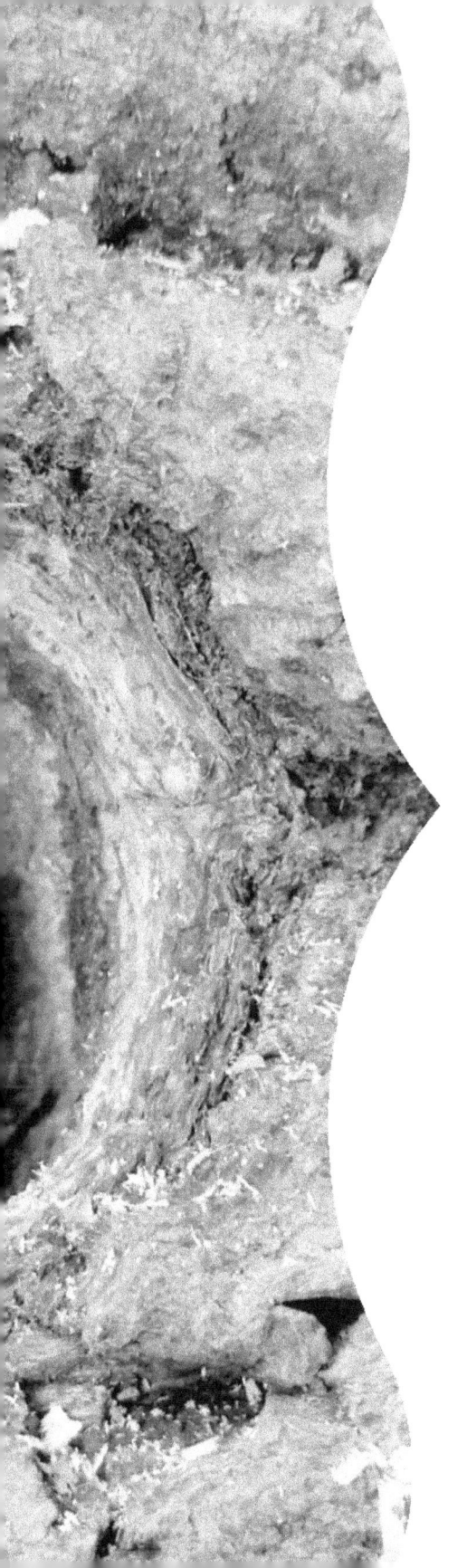

A pit is a pit;
it makes no
difference who
puts you into it

A ram leading a pride will turn brave lions into sheep

Don't be surprised
if your bird
doesn't fly
if you keep
it locked in
a cage

Eagles have no business in chicken squabbles

If you consistently ignore what's on your doorstep, it eventually will enter your house

If you don't
learn you'll
be taught

If you keep shifting the goalpost, you'll never be able to score

If you're a go-getter, you've got to go get it!

If your dream is in the sea, learn to swim; if your dream is in the sky, learn to fly; pursue your dream!

In life, it's not about having more; it's about doing more with what you have

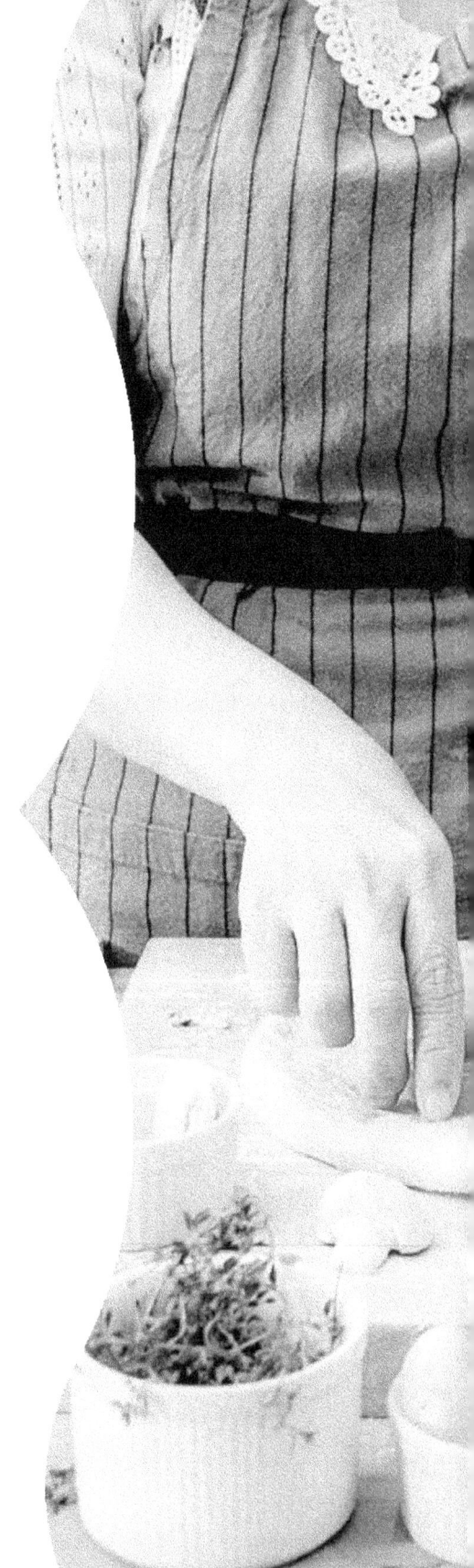

It's impossible to run with people who insist on crawling

Leadership is not about the number of followers you have; it's about rising to that occasion when that occasion arises

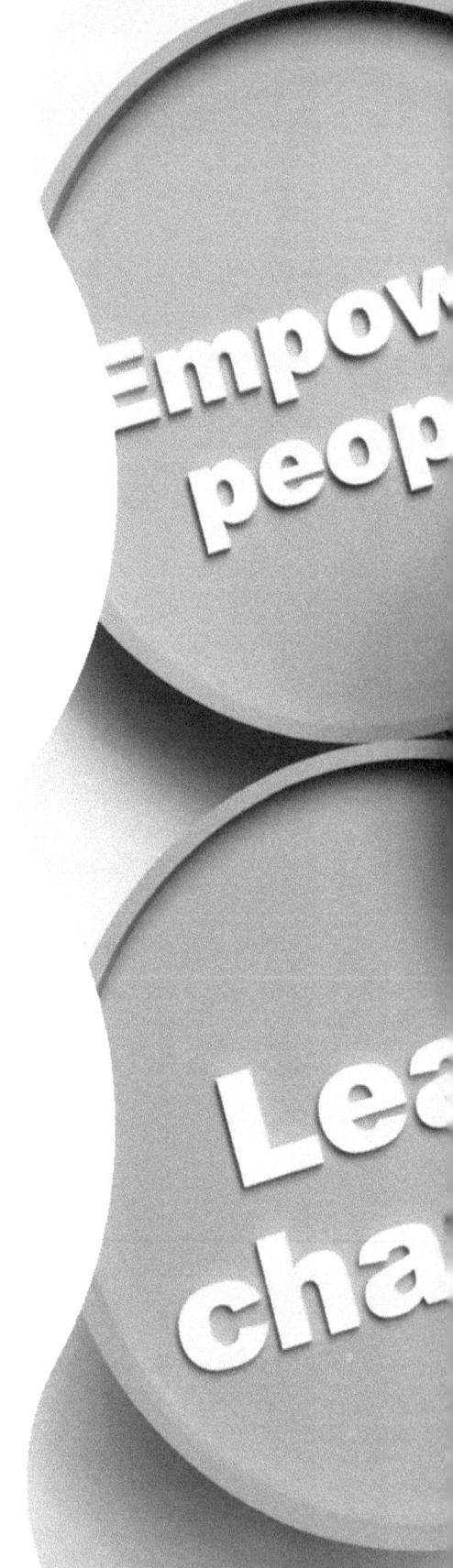

Learn to ignore the subject but pass the course

Life without learning is not living

Motivation
gets you going,
passion keeps
you growing,
but it's persistence
that gets you there

No one person can do every single thing, but every single person can do one thing

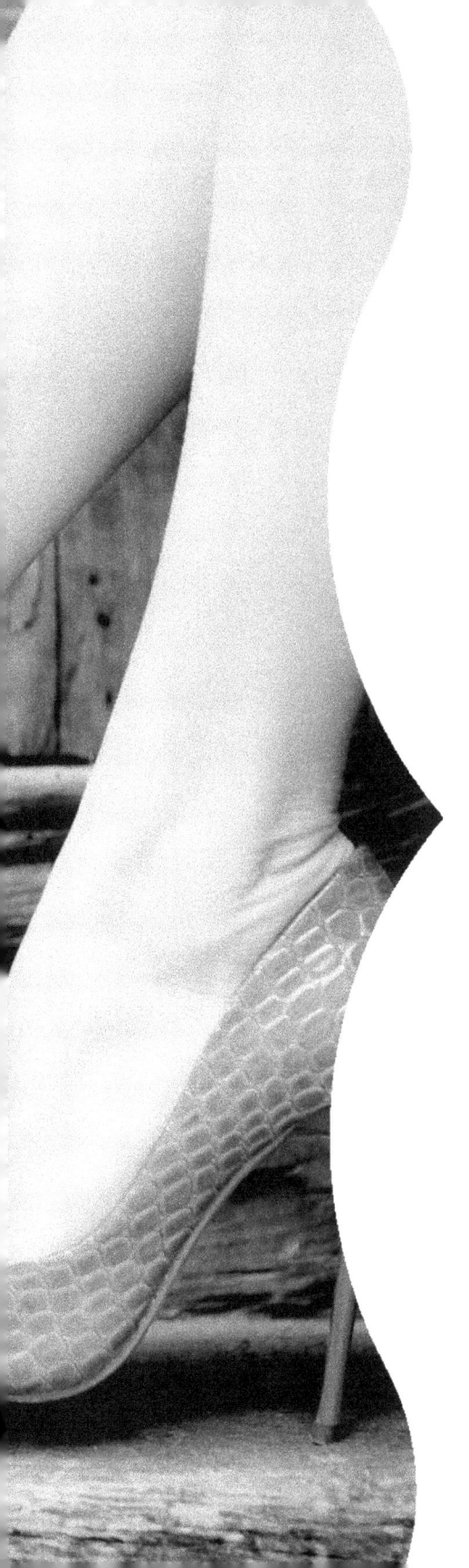

No matter how expensive the shoes, they still have to touch the ground

Plan your journey even if you don't have a ride

Safe is not spectacular!

Sometimes to build it up you've got to tear it down; construction often requires demolition

Stepping stones may look like stumbling blocks

The doctor has the medicine, and the medicine has the doctor

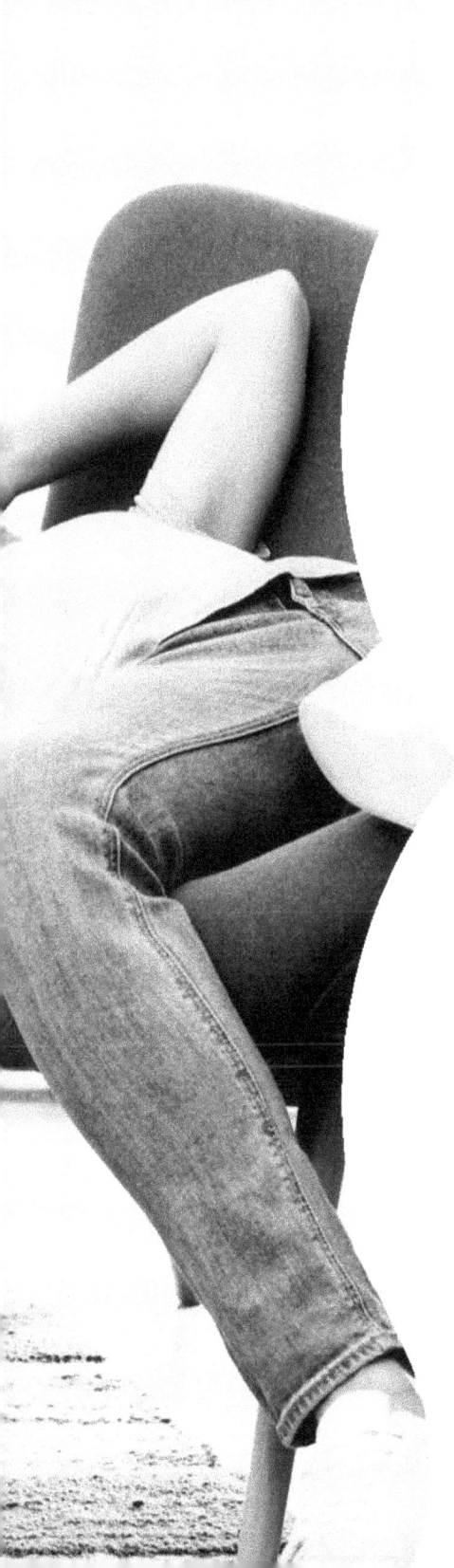

There's no point in asking for help if you're doing nothing

There's no point in falling on your knees when really you should be rolling up your sleeves

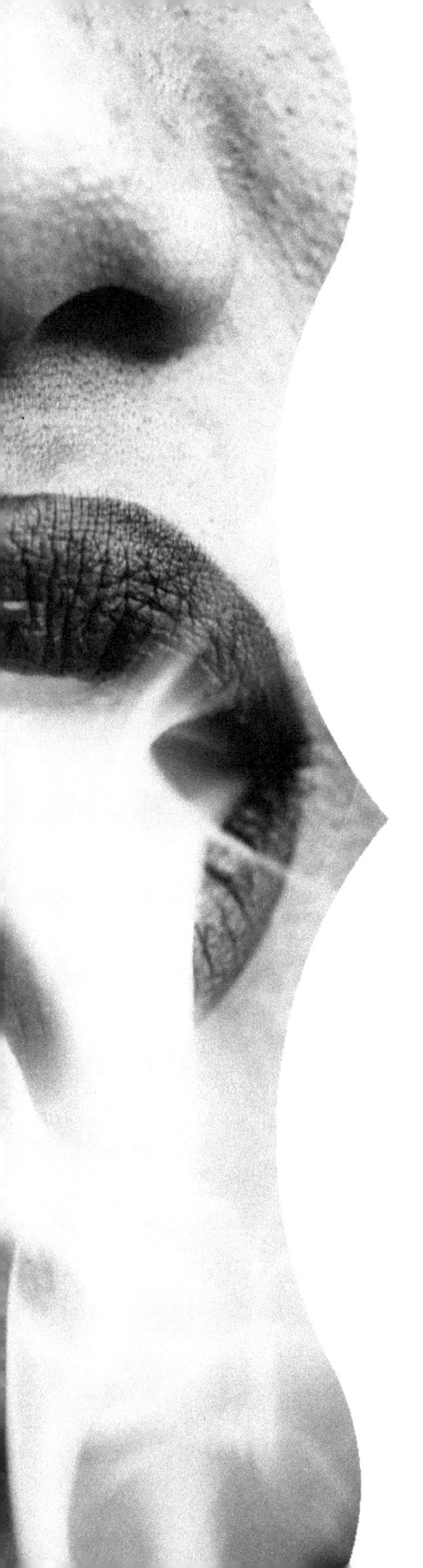

The ultimate remedy for a bad habit is a final diagnosis

We can mother, and we can mentor, but it's when we model that we make the greatest impact

When tiger
steps up
poodle
steps back

You can't sit on it and expect it to move

Part II – MIND

The mind encompasses our cognitive and intellectual capacities. It includes our thoughts, emotions, perceptions, memories, reasoning abilities, and consciousness. The mind is responsible for processing information, analyzing experiences, and forming beliefs. It's where our inner dialogues occur, and it's closely tied to our sense of self. The mind also plays a crucial role in shaping our behaviors, decisions, and responses to the world around us.

Mental well-being affects physical and spiritual well-being: Our thoughts and emotions can have a direct impact on our physical health. Stress, for example, can lead to physical ailments. A healthy mind can also be more receptive to spiritual growth and exploration.

The idea of these three components—body, mind, and spirit— being interconnected emphasizes the idea that a person is not simply a sum of isolated parts, but rather a holistic and integrated whole. This perspective suggests that the well-being of one aspect can impact the well-being of the others.

Every lioness
wants her lion
to roar but not
at her

Everything means nothing until it's grounded in reality

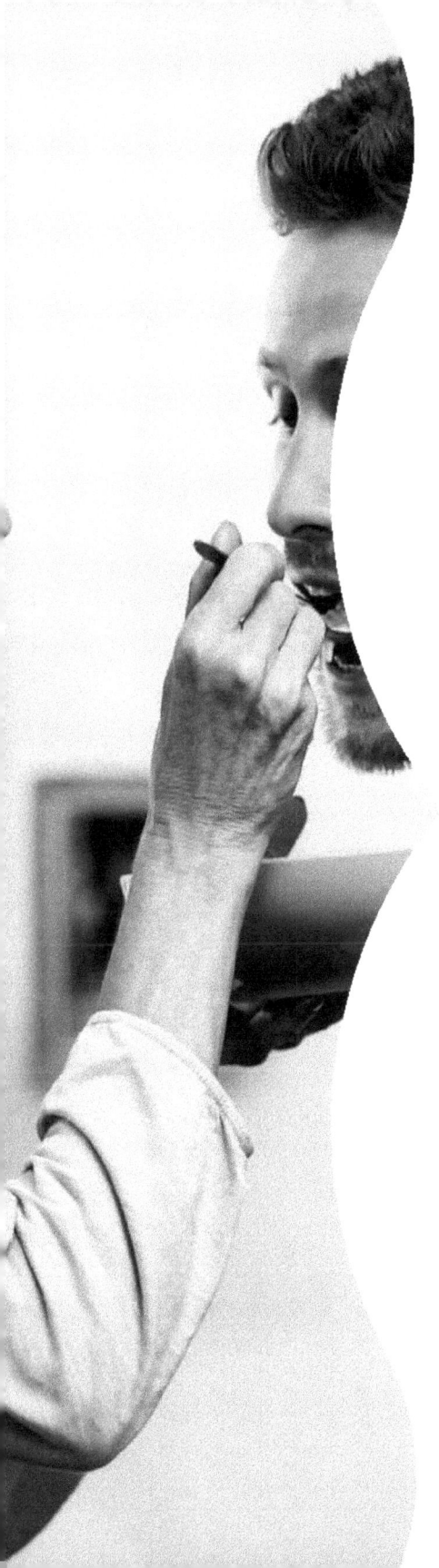

If the enemy is feeding you, rest assured that he is also feeding off you

If you build yourself a prison, you shouldn't be surprised if you find yourself behind bars

If you can't do it alone, do it together; and if you can't go together, go it alone

If you can't
see it,
then you
won't see it

If you don't have
what it takes,
take what
you have

If you don't know, you don't know; but when you wise up you must rise up!

If you insist on complicating life, it will simplify & may even cancel you; when all is said and done, life is a simple equation

If you're being pulled in different directions, you shouldn't be surprised if you go to pieces

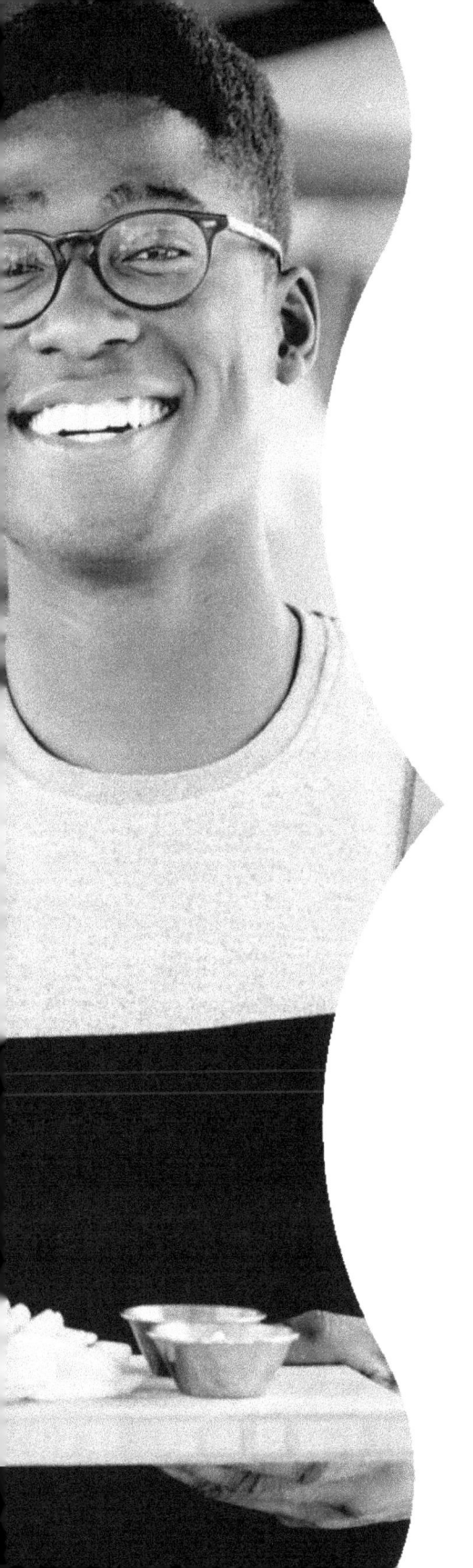

It is better to
walk away
limping than
to stand firm
in
the wrong
place

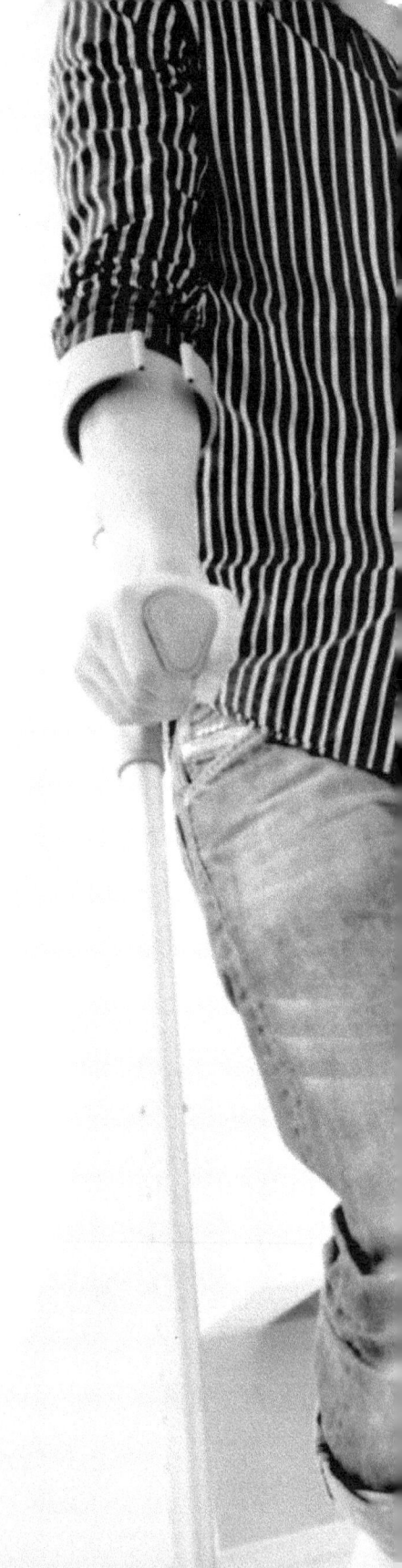

It's okay to be different because in reality, you are

Life is just for learning!

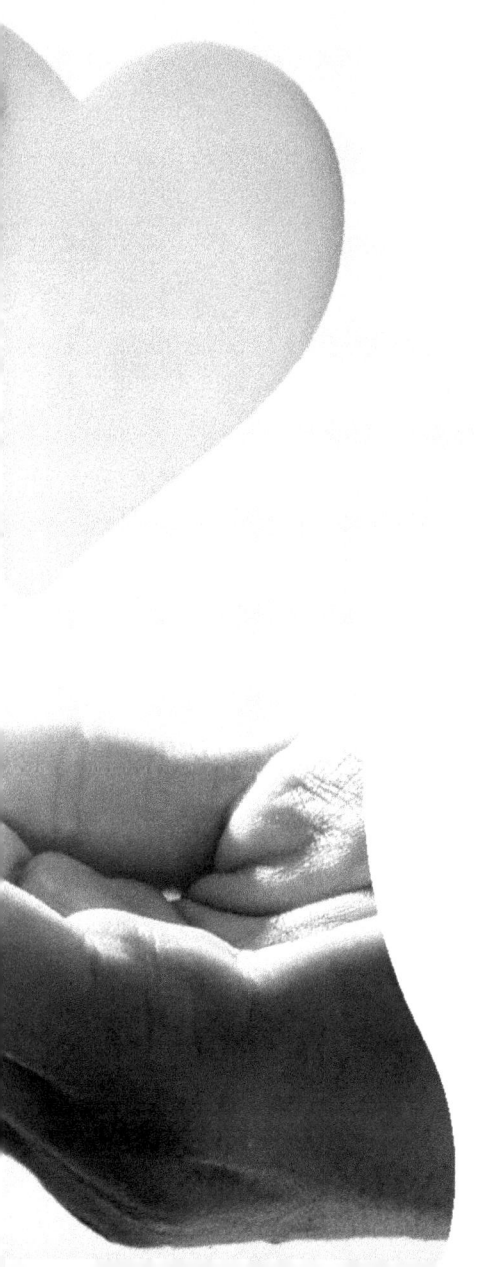

Love says yes, and love says no;
love holds on and love lets go.
Love is being, and love is doing;
love is really understanding

Sometimes
it takes
separation
to create unity

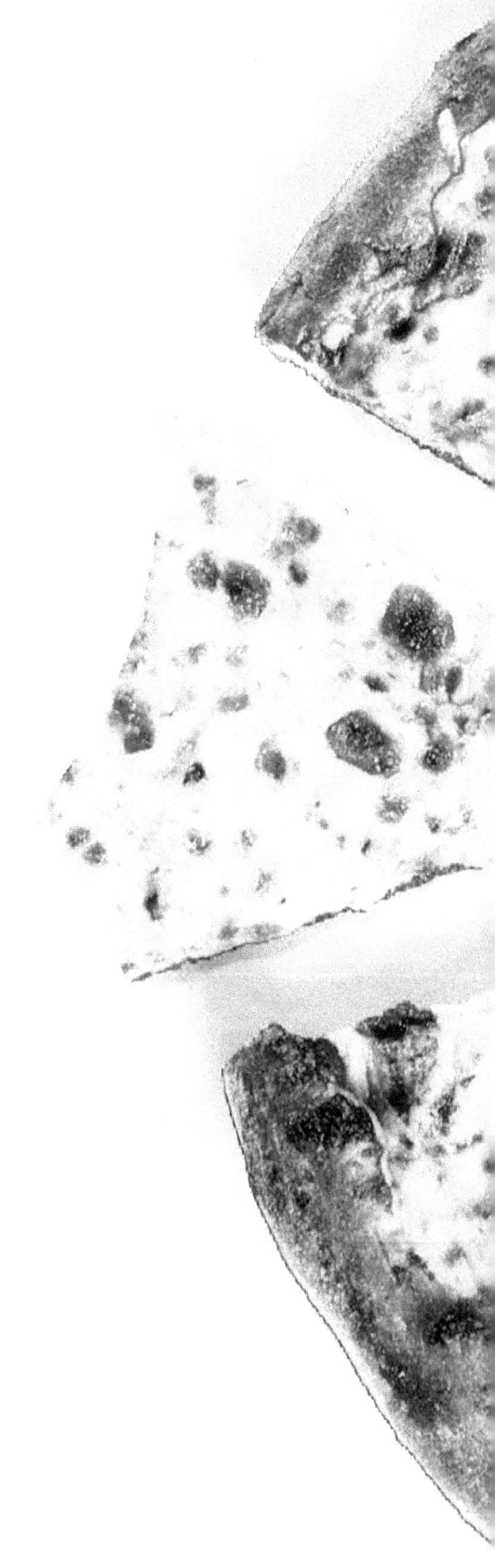

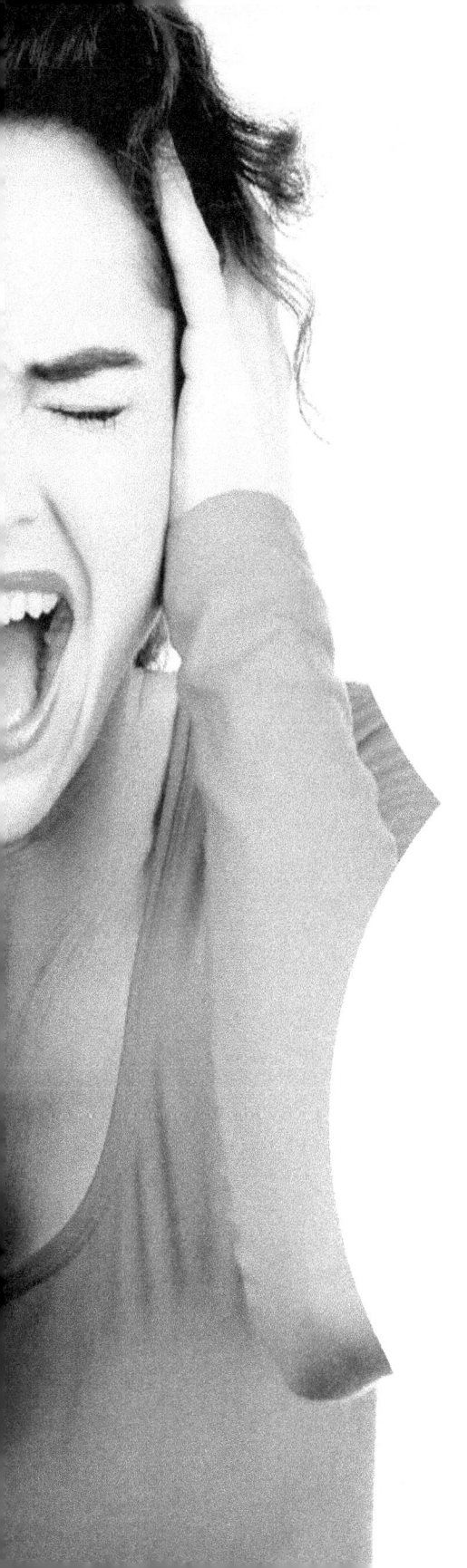

Sometimes it's harder to do nothing

Sometimes, the best way to speak to someone is to say nothing

Sometimes, we have to walk away from a good thing in order to access a great thing

Sometimes, you have to protect yourself from people you love

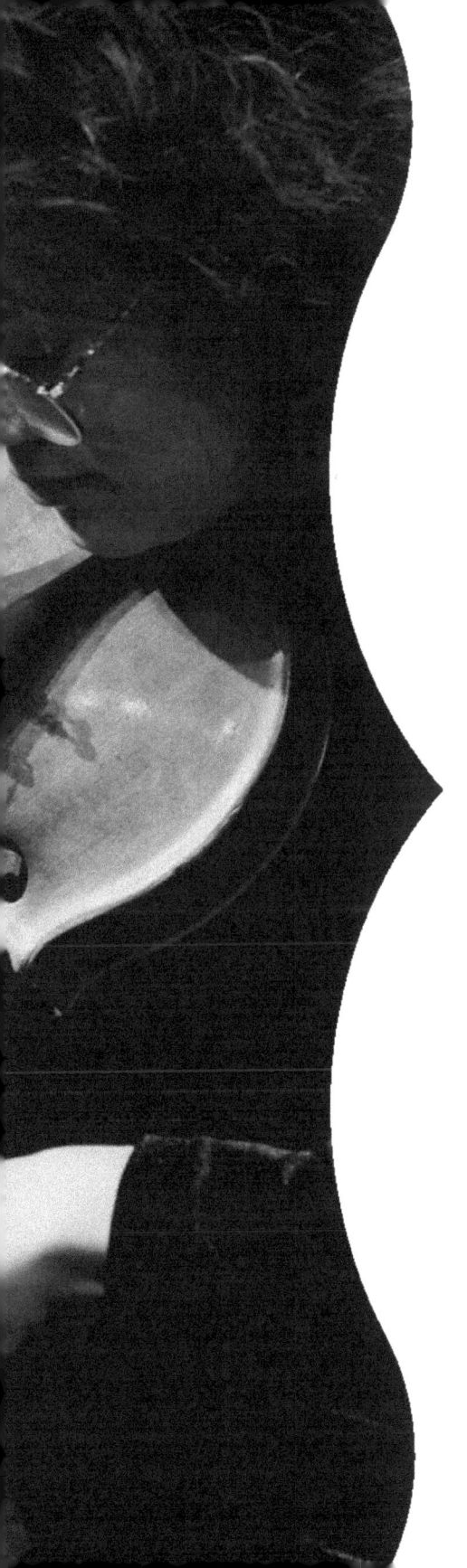

Talent without ambition makes for wasted gifting

The fact that one is quiet doesn't mean he has nothing to say

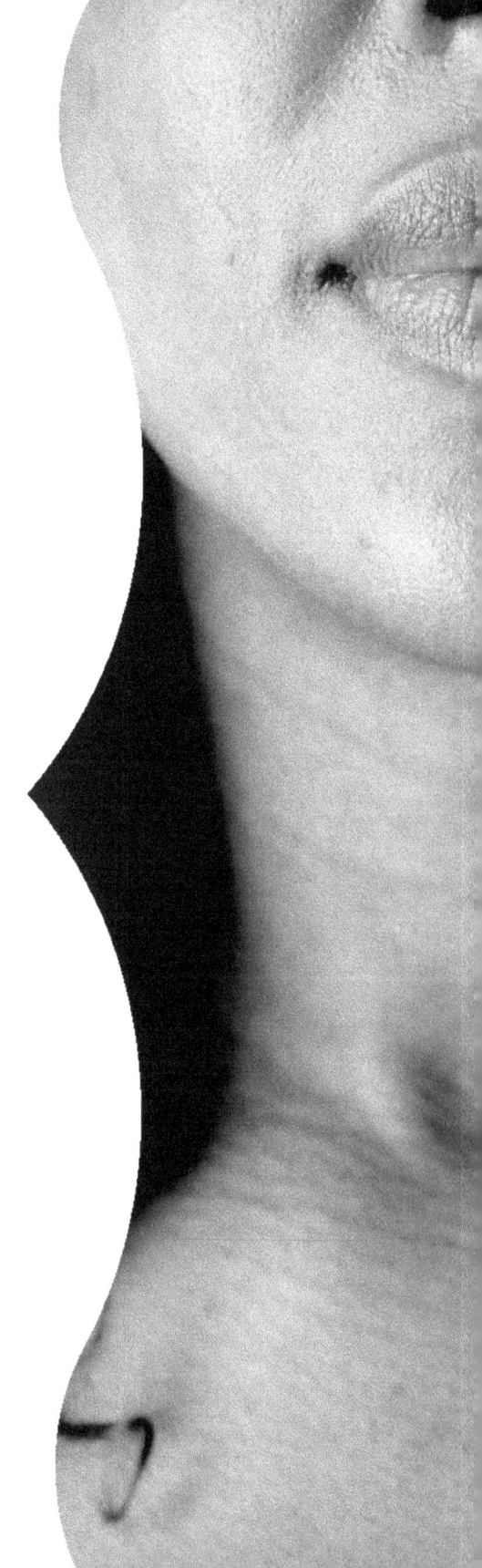

The road to success
Is dogged by urges to quit;
don't let the dogs out!

The same hands that gesture 'hello' are the same hands that wave 'goodbye'

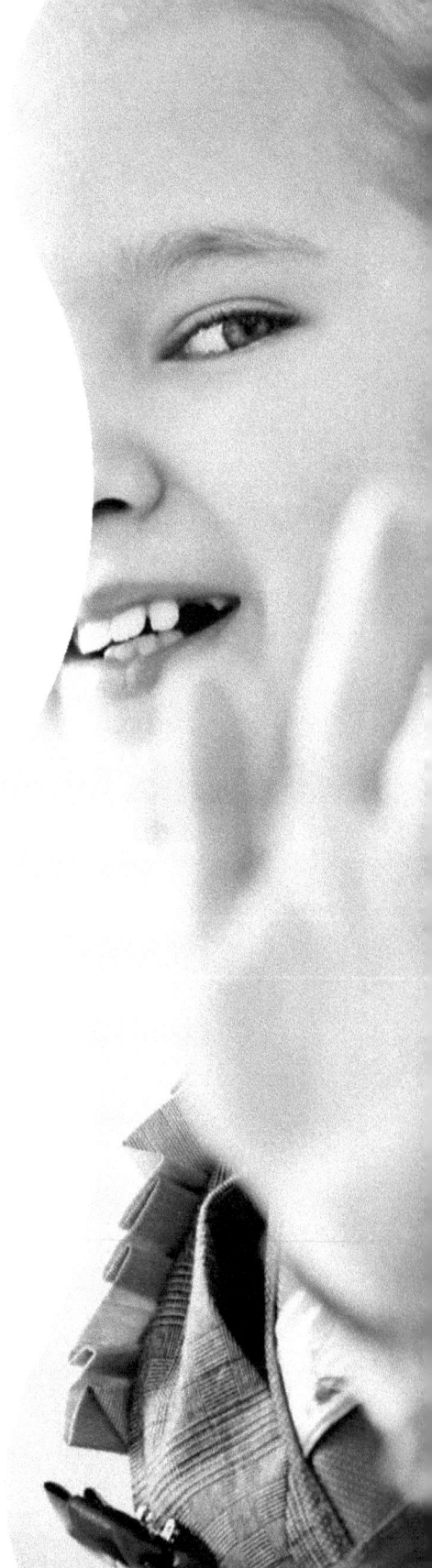

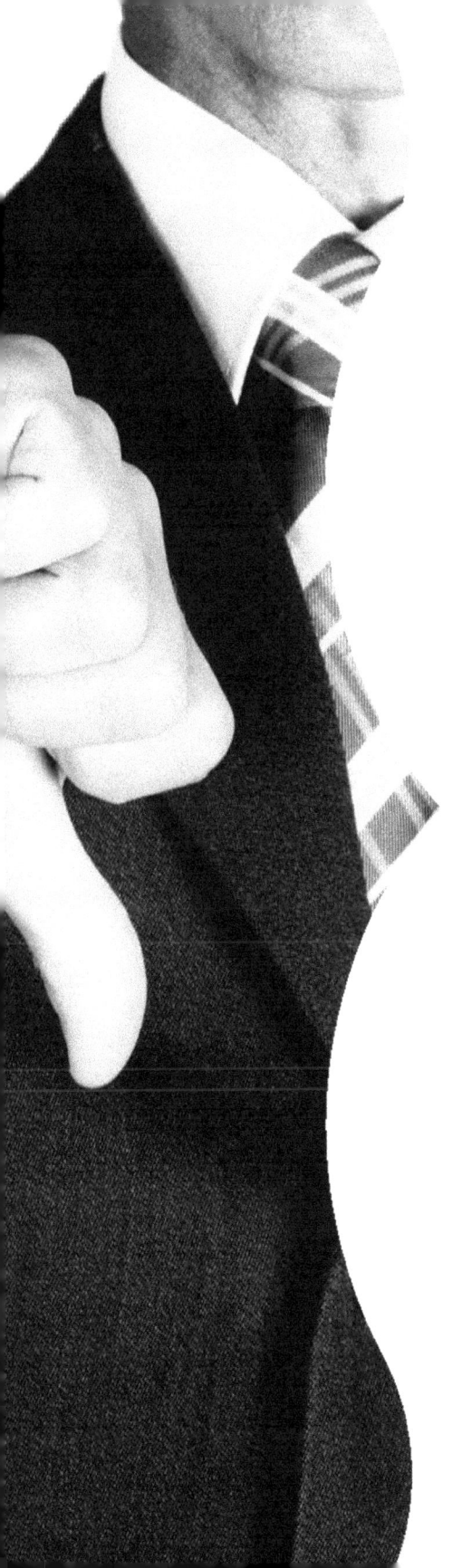

There can be
no dishonor
worse than that
meted out to
oneself

Those who
live
in fire have no
fear of heat

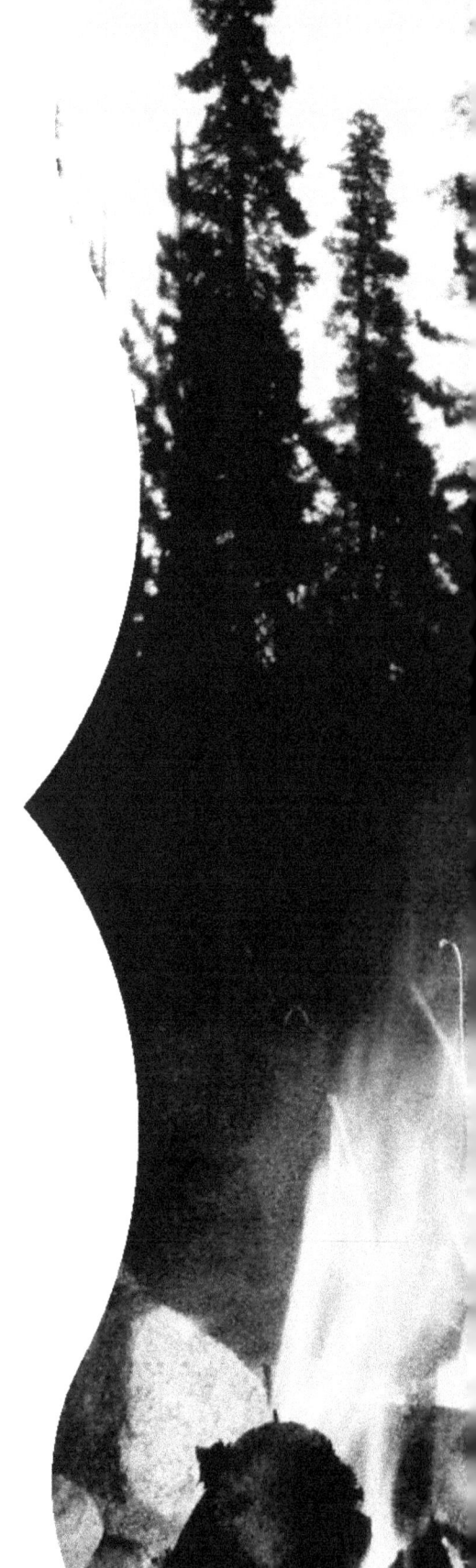

Try to be all
things
to all men,
and you'll end up
being nothing to
anyone

Walking away
is not the same
as leaving

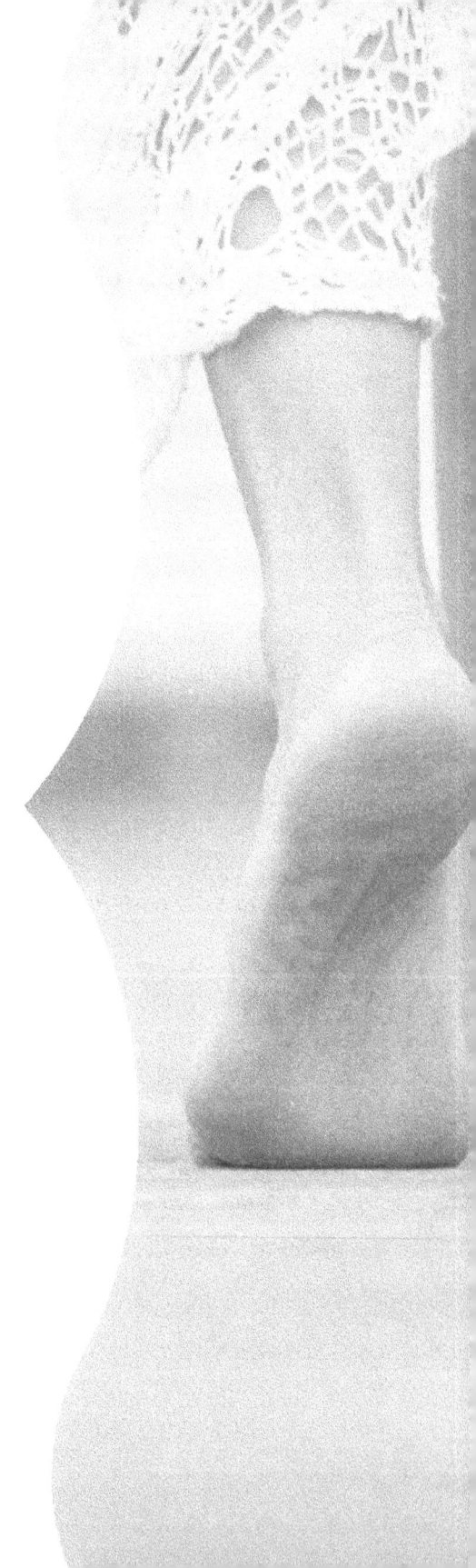

What we earn gives us a living but it is what we learn that gives us a life

When you
know there's no
safety net,
you're
careful how
you leap

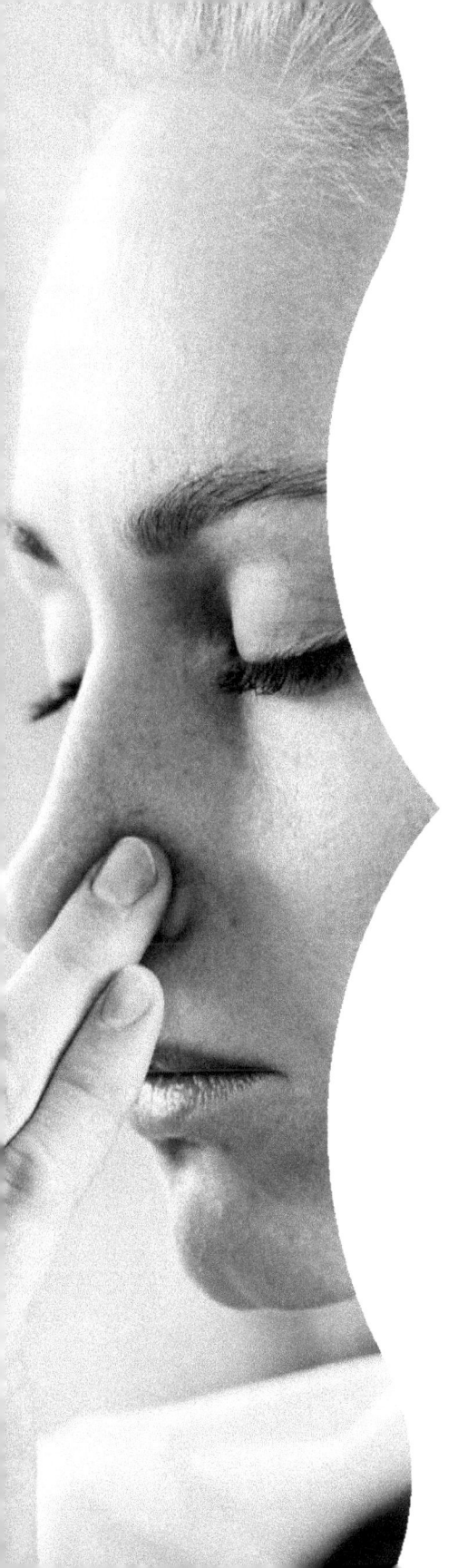

You can hold your breath for so long; but at some point, you've got to exhale

You can't
court war
and expect to
marry peace

Part III – SPIRIT

The concept of spirit or soul delves into the more intangible and transcendent aspect of our existence. It is often associated with our deepest essence, inner values, purpose, and connection to something greater than ourselves. The spirit is sometimes thought to be the source of our creativity, intuition, and the capacity to experience profound meaning and spirituality. It's the part of us that seeks purpose and transcends the limitations of the material world.

Spiritual well-being affects mental and physical well-being: Having a sense of purpose, connection to others, and a deeper understanding of life's meaning can contribute to emotional resilience and mental clarity. Spiritual practices like meditation and mindfulness have been shown to have positive effects on both mental and physical health.

In essence, the concept of being body, mind, and spirit highlights the intricate interplay between these different dimensions of human existence. Nurturing all three aspects can lead to a more balanced, fulfilling, and holistic life.

As a human being,
here comes a time
when
you've got to
stop doing and
start being

A snake may
glitter
but a snake
is not gold

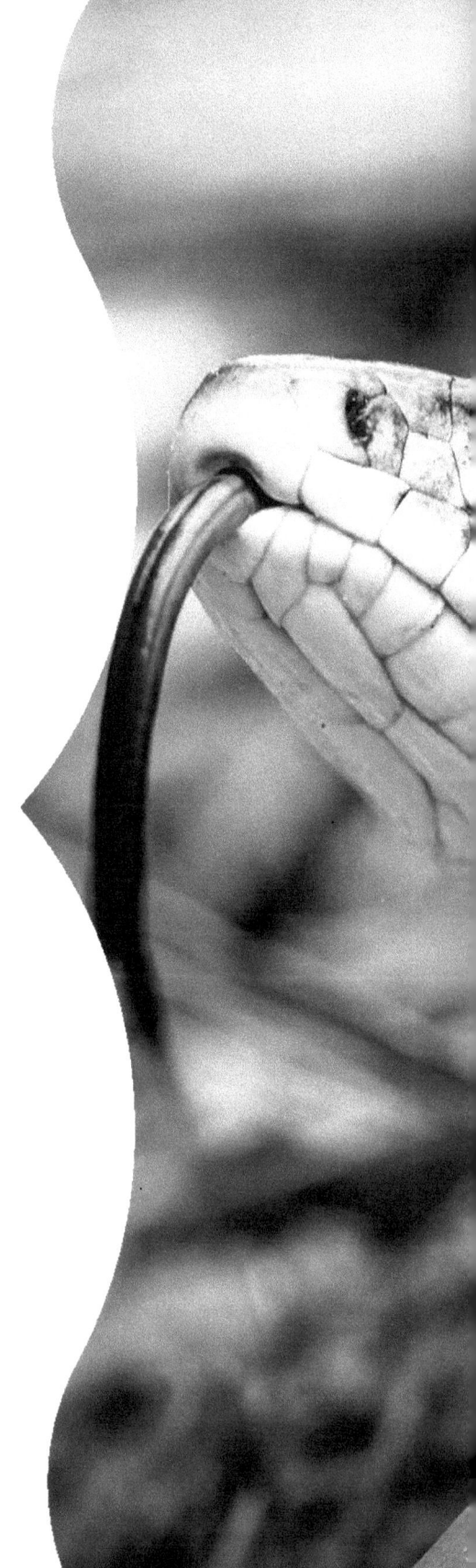

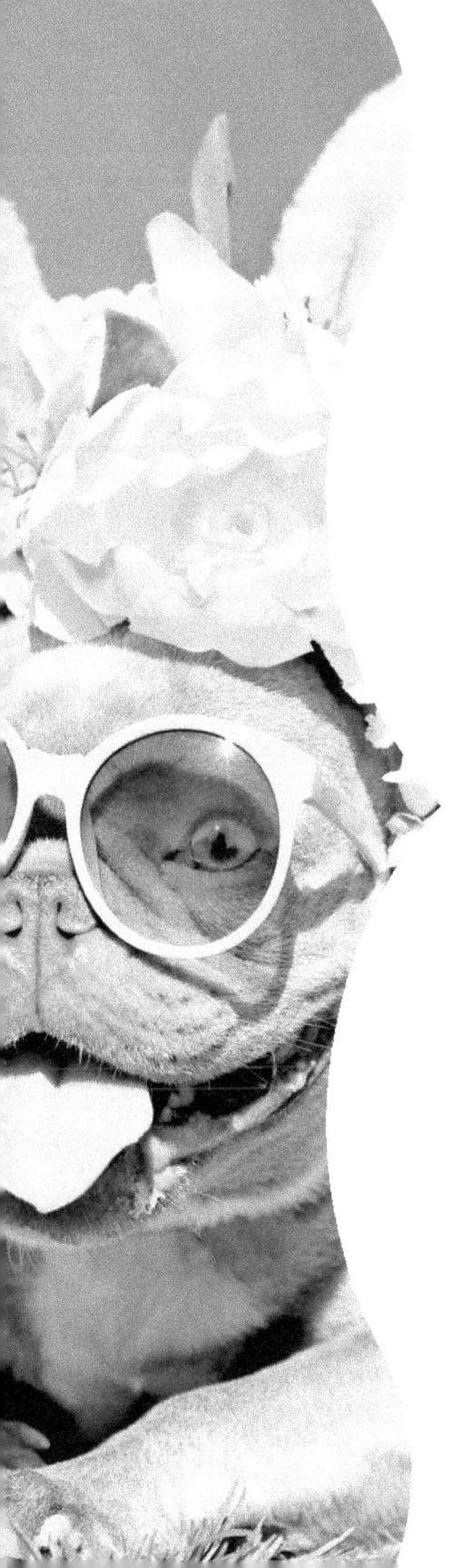

A well-dressed
lie may be sexier
than the naked
truth but
nothing leaves
you as exposed
like a well-
dressed lie

As you don't
know what's
around
the corner,
be careful how
you drive

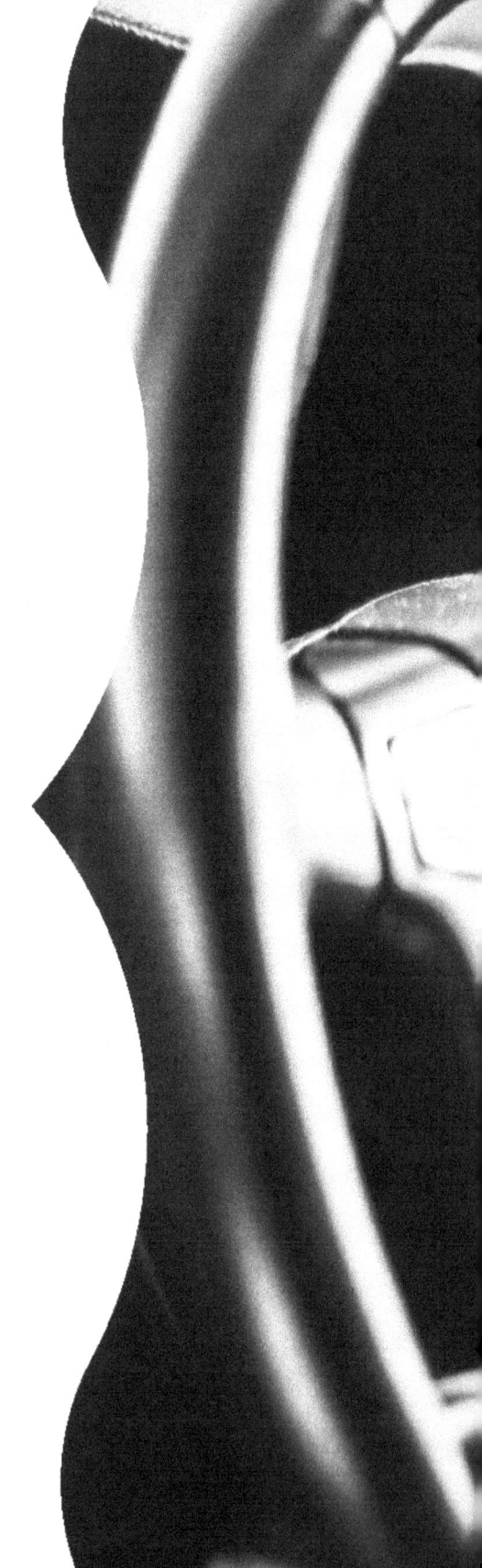

Cows don't coo
and doves
don't moo;
in all you are,
say and do,
be real and true
to you

Grey is neither
black nor white
but grey is
black and white

If you don't share
when you have
little, you won't
share when you
have much

If you find
yourself
without,
go find
yourself
within

If you flirt with
the devil
don't be surprised
if
you find
yourself in hell

If you have a stone, you can throw it but you can choose not to

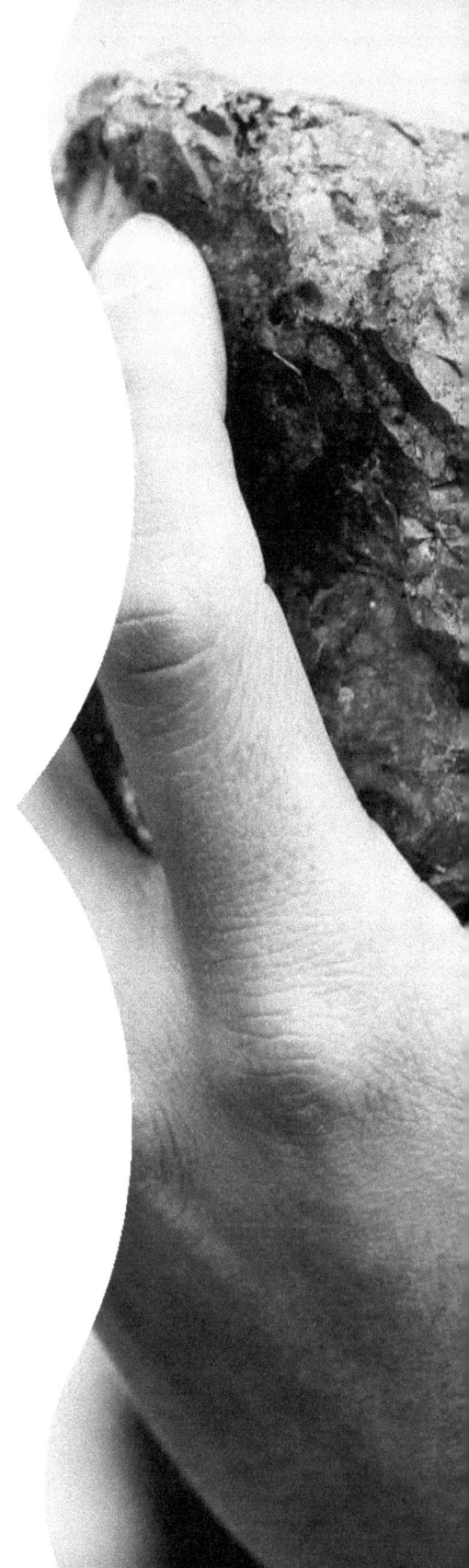

If you have
freedom,
free someone,
if you have power,
empower
someone;
if you have light,
enlighten
someone;
if you have
energy, energize
someone

If you insist on fighting God, you will lose

If you wander
too far from
your source,
you're bound to
lose your way

If you're broke challenge your mind; if you're broken, challenge your heart

In order to move
forward
sometimes
you've got to
stand still

It's not every response that is an answer

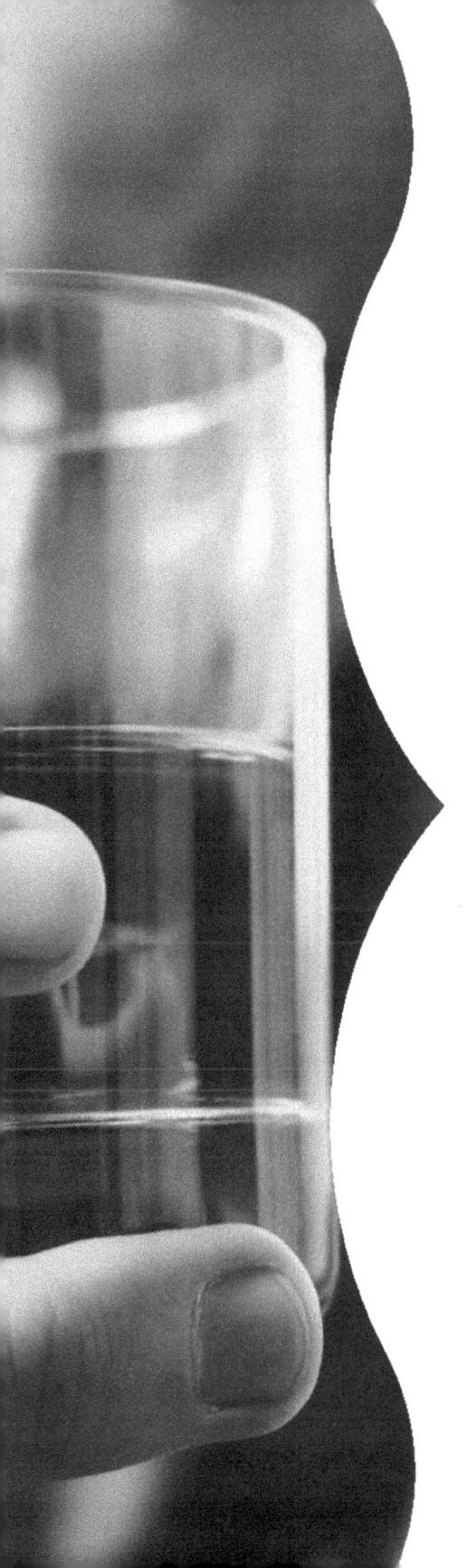

It's hard to save
a man
who's in love
with his demons

Just because you have less doesn't mean you're worth any less

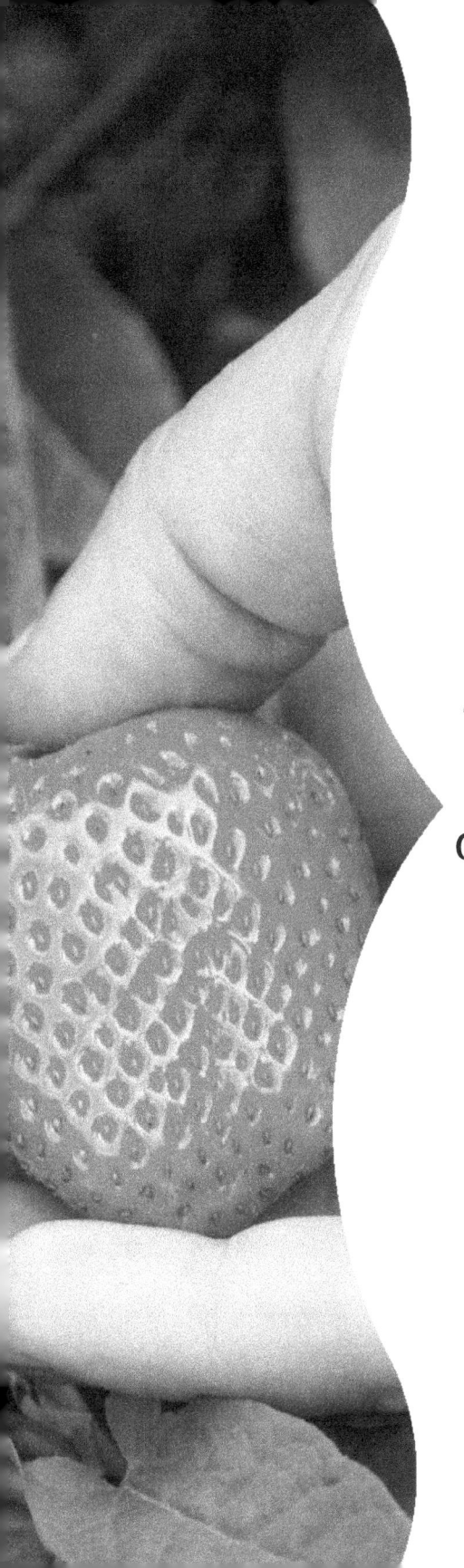

Just because your
hand can reach it
doesn't mean that
you must pick it

Life has its ups
and downs, but
no one has to
be down for
me to be up

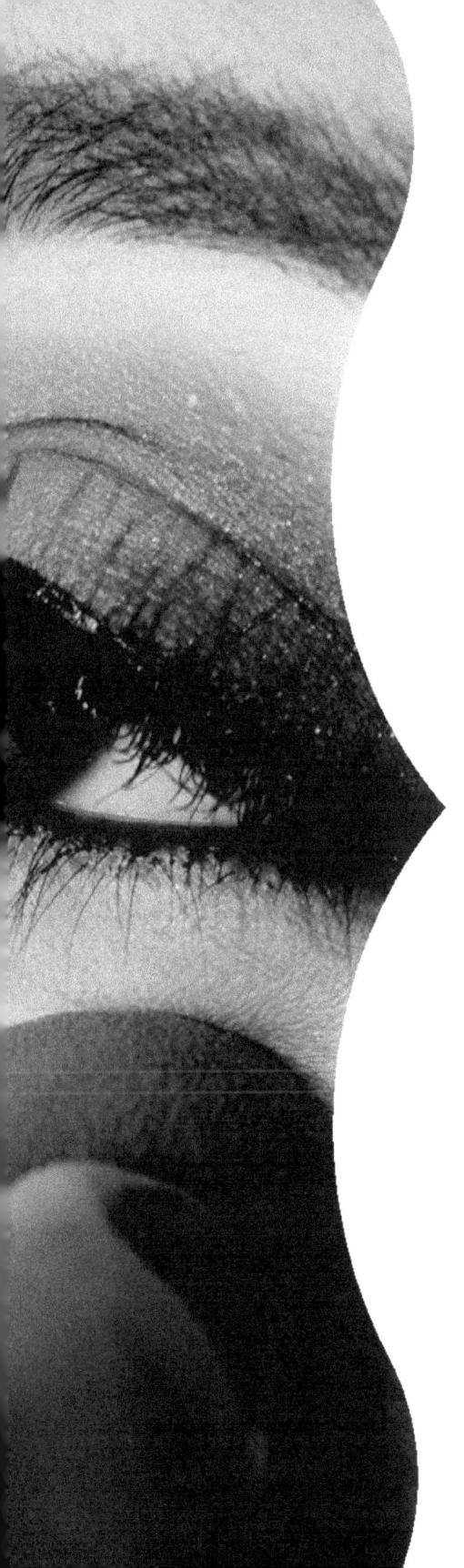

No amount of powder can puff away an ugly character

No one starts from nothing, as no one was born with nothing

Peace is a deliberate action

'Silence'
and
'Peace'
are not
synonymous

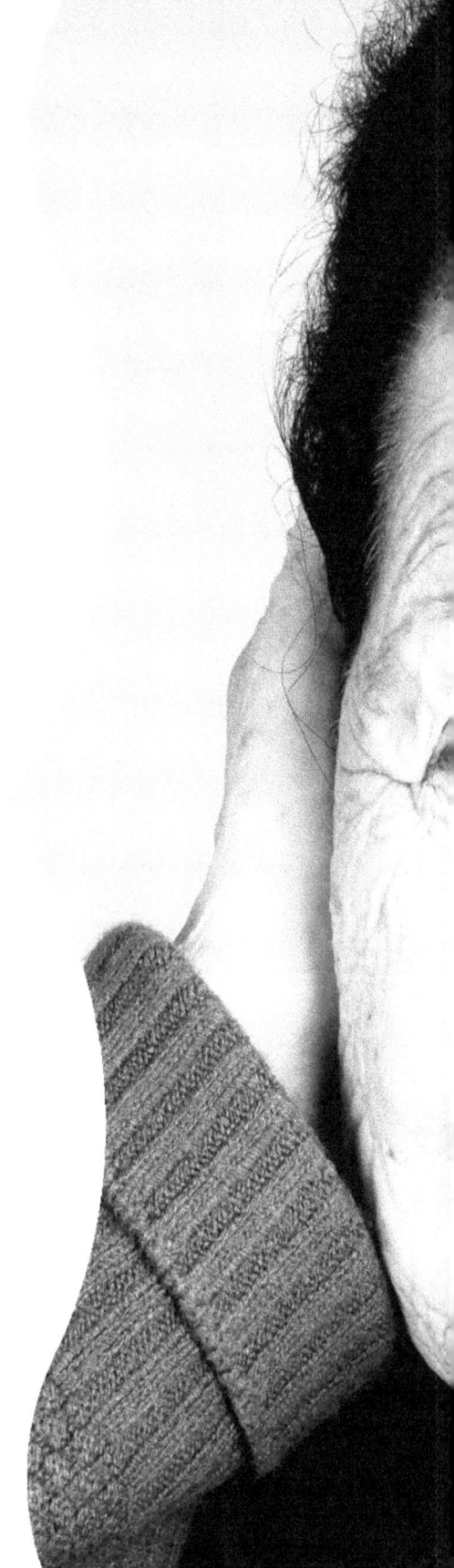

Sometimes,
all you have
to do is be

Sow
where you
don't expect
to reap

Standing at the altar does not alter your standing

The greatest thing you can ever do is become who you're meant to be

The journey of a thousand miles begins in the mind

The pain is greater when it's later

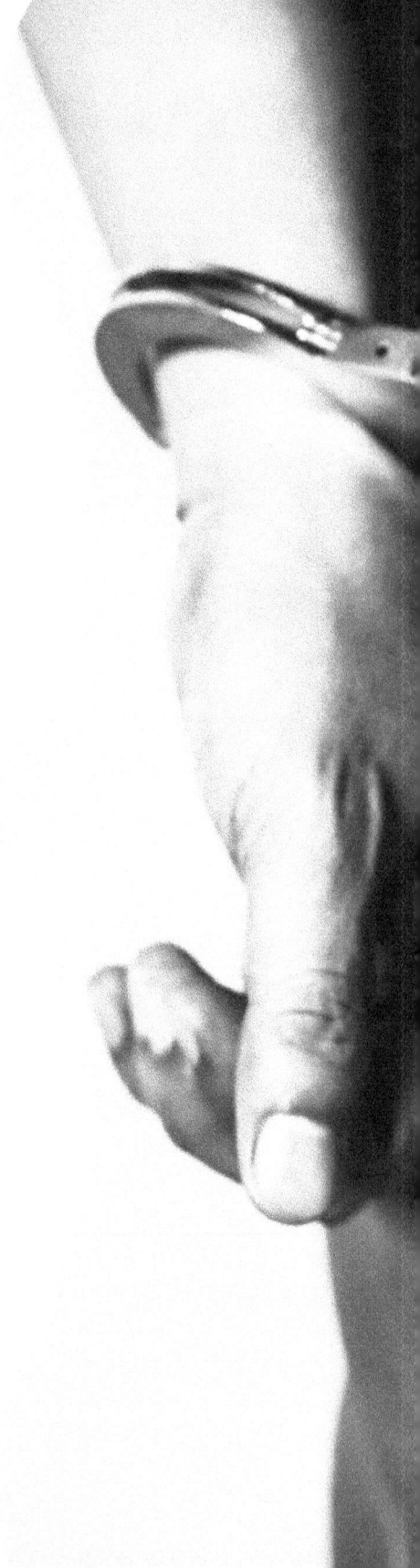

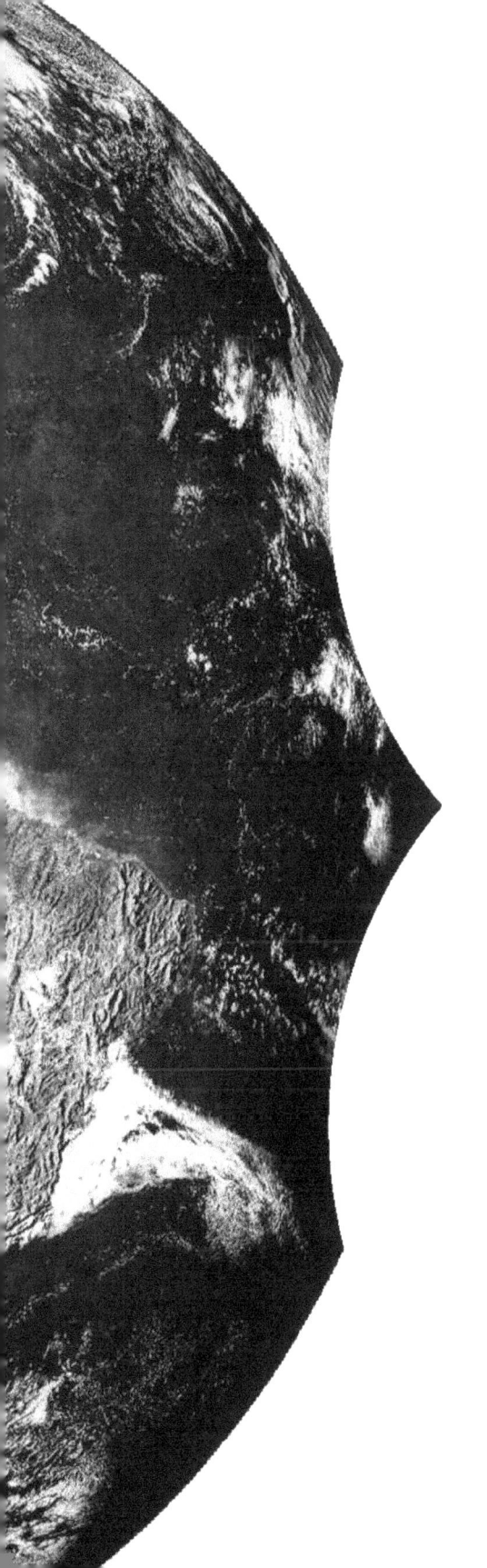

The world goes around and comes back around; sooner or later, each shall have his turn

Until you find yourself, no one can find you

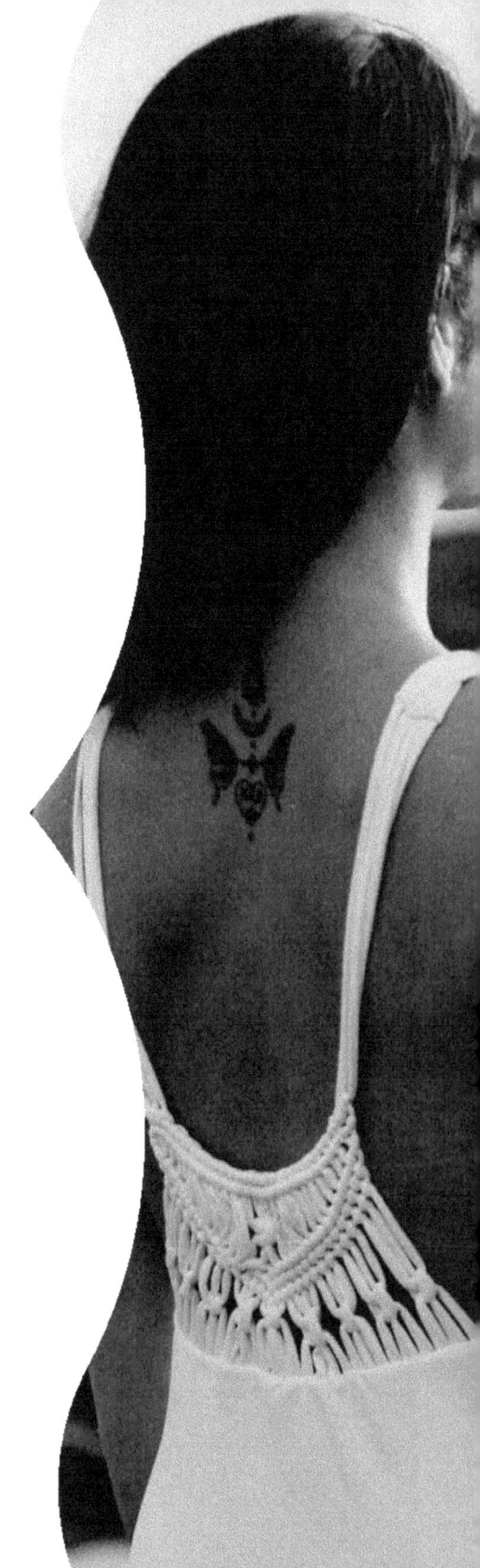

When people find
all that they want
in the light they
start to look
in the dark

When the ball
falls into the
gutter,
it's time to
get out of the
game

Who you are
determines what
you do,
and what you do
reveals who you
are

You can choose to be bitter or choose to be better by changing a letter that you write to yourself

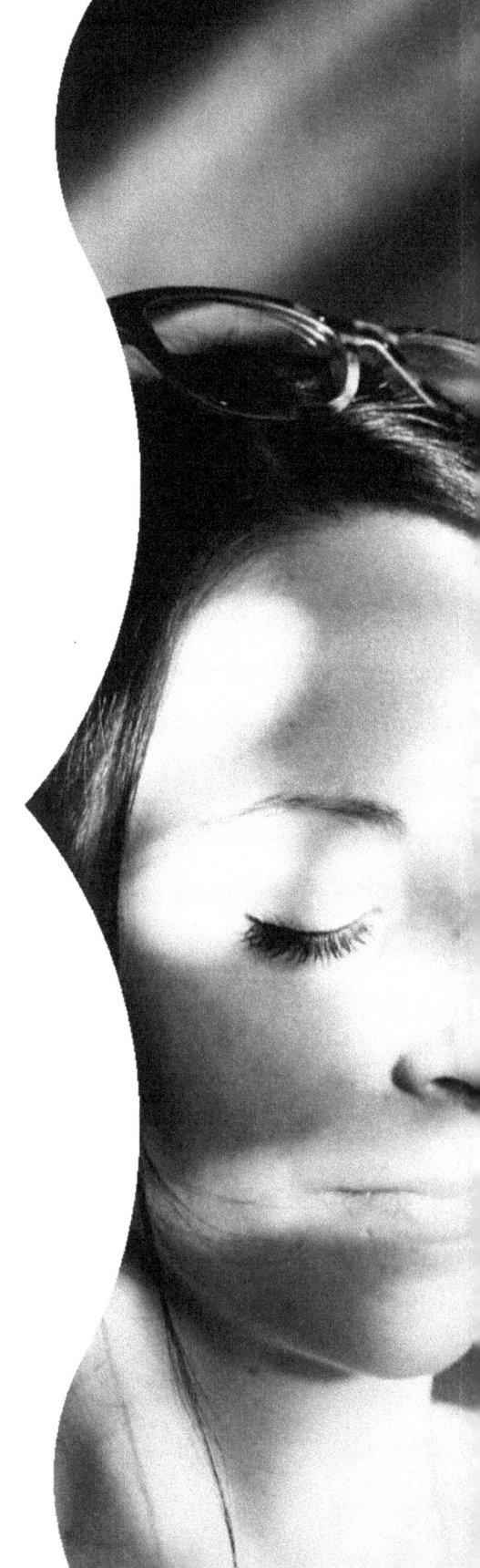

You can't sow discord and reap concord

You can't use heart surgery to treat a head injury

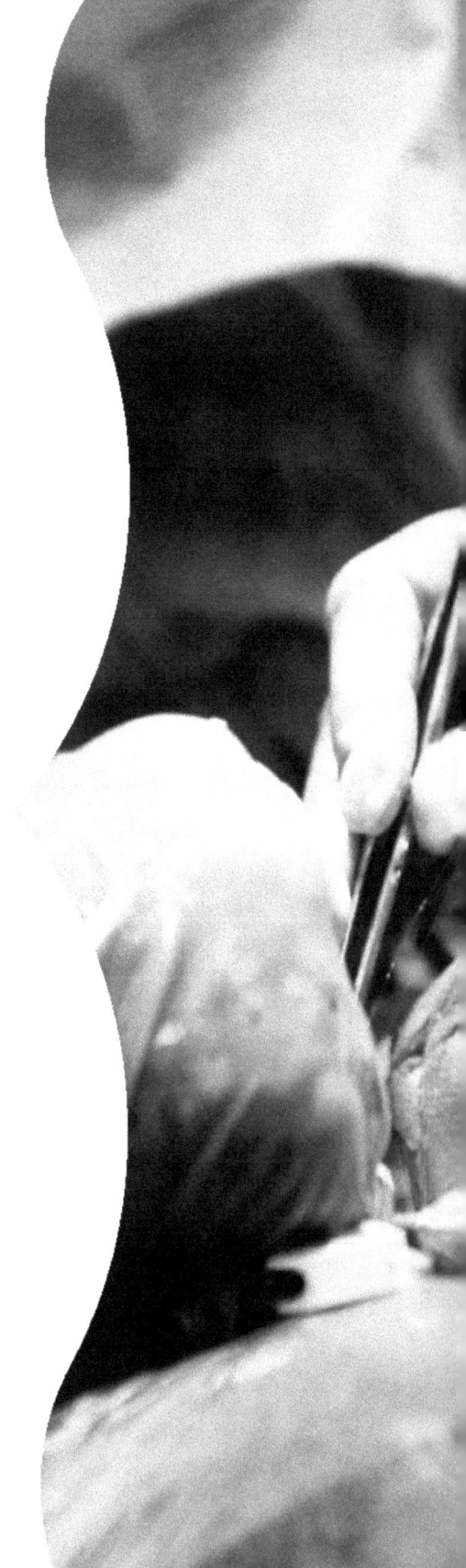

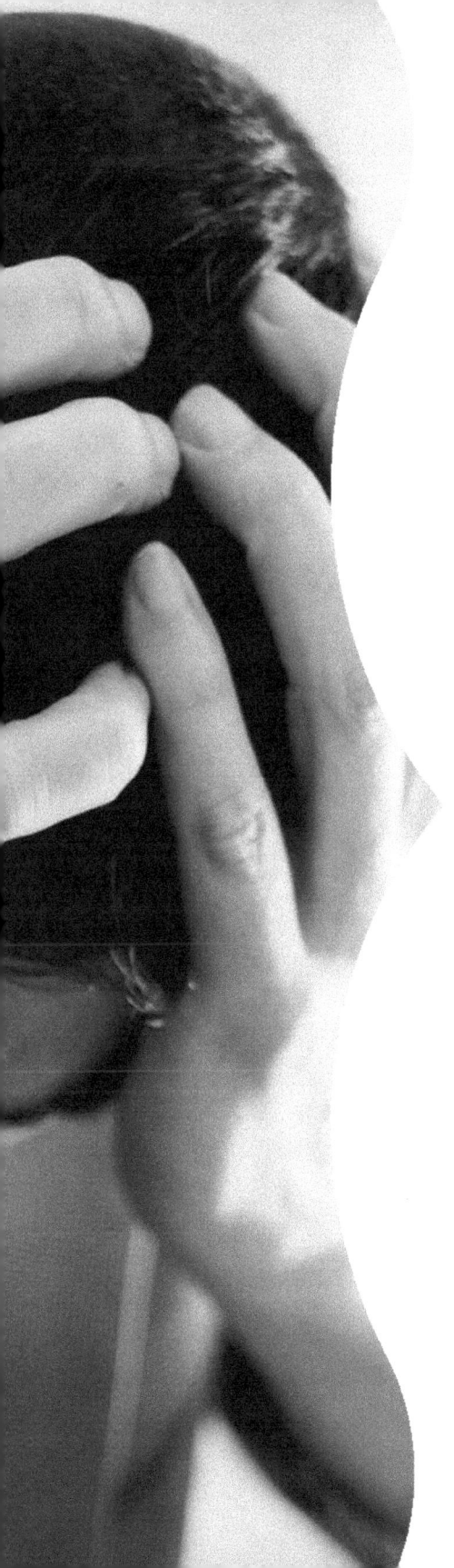

You may be helpless but be not hopeless; for where there's hope, there's life

CONCLUSION

As we close the chapters of "101 Original Inspirational Quotes That Make You Think," we find ourselves not at an end but a new beginning—a beginning that transcends the boundaries of these pages and extends into the vast landscape of your life. This book has been a journey of exploration, self-discovery, and a celebration of the profound wisdom that resides within us all.

Throughout these pages, we've ventured into the realm of originality, where each quote is a beacon of light, illuminating our path toward personal growth, critical thinking, and meaningful leadership. These are not just words on paper; they are sparks of inspiration, invitations to introspection, and catalysts for transformation.

In this book, you've encountered themes that resonate with the human experience—leadership, resilience, empathy, ethics, innovation, and the pursuit of purpose. These themes are not isolated; they are interconnected threads that weave the fabric of a meaningful life. I've shared these quotes, hoping they resonate with you, challenge your perspectives, and ignite curiosity and empathy within you. But remember, the power of these quotes lies not in their mere reading but in their application.

The journey of personal and professional growth is ongoing; these original insights are your companions. They are tools in your toolkit, guiding you toward innovative solutions, ethical choices, and a leadership style rooted in authenticity.

As you close this book, I encourage you to carry the wisdom you've found here into your daily life. Let it inform your decisions, guide your interactions, and inspire you to become the best version of yourself. Share these insights with others, for in sharing, we multiply the potential for positive change.

May these quotes remain a source of inspiration and empowerment long after you've turned the final page. May they continue to challenge your thinking, nurture your resilience, and deepen your understanding and wisdom.

Your leadership journey is boundless, filled with opportunities to make a difference, inspire change, and lead with purpose.

Thank you for embarking on this path with me. Here's to a future defined by critical thinking, ethical leadership, and a commitment to making the world a better place—one thoughtful decision at a time.

Other Books You'll Love

EMPOWERED
https://www.amazon.com/dp/B096SQ4XPW

The book, "Empowered", is the precursor to the present book. Empowered contains 120 divinely inspired quotes similar to those contained in the present text.

That book too can be used to inspire creative thinking in various settings ranging from the family room to the board room.

LIFE LESSONS FROM A BOUNCING BALL https://amzn.to/3AUCH06

There is wisdom to be gained from playing. This book, based on a simple indoor ball game, is packed with life lessons that stimulates thought, imagination and creative thinking.

Researchers have found that play isn't just about having fun; it also reduces stress and enhances our overall well-being. This book shows that there is much to learn from simple activities.

ABOUT THE AUTHOR

Andrea Campbell, MBA, MA, is a social entrepreneur, linguist, and inspirational writer. Since publishing her first book in 2010, Andrea has released several bestselling books and articles about special needs parenting and personal development.

Over the years, she has focused on empowering vulnerable people through education and inspiration. As the mother of a child with special educational needs, she is particularly keen on working with families to enable their disabled children to aspire higher and achieve their potential. She also developed the Pocket Learner–a set of multi-award-winning innovative educational resources for parents, caregivers and educators of children with special educational needs.

Andrea has also published various inspirational coloring books, journals, logs and activity books to empower and inspire people everywhere.

Andrea resides with her family in London, UK, where she continues to impact through her writing, creative exploits, training programs, coaching, philanthropy, and inspirational speaking.

Connect with Andrea at andrea@acttrainingco.com.

www.ingramcontent.com/pod-product-compliance
Lightning Source LLC
Chambersburg PA
CBHW041301240426
43661CB00010B/982